Event Planner

How to Start a Full Service
Event Planning Business

By J. H. Dies

A Newbiz Playbook Publication

FIRST EDITION ISBN-13: 978-1979955119

This book comes with a complete set of electronic tools, templates, and customizable forms. See page 50 for the details on how to obtain them.

For my family, the answer to my why

Understanding Your "Product"

The fundamental truth about event planning is that the product is, for those who hire you, a dream. Many of the people looking for your expertise have imagined this moment for a substantial part of their lives, or from the time of the birth of a child. Your task is to deliver that perfect day. One of the biggest mistakes that new wedding and event planners make is to try to use low prices, or the perception of discounted value to attract customers. Your customers don't want the cheap option, and what's more they will be less likely to hire someone offering it.

People who hire professionals for this service are looking for an elite experience, and for you that means incredible responsiveness. You provide a cell phone. You answer emails within hours if not minutes. For that your customers will pay a premium. Your image, dress, tone, and interactions create this experience.

Nordstrom's products are expensive, even more expensive than other stores by a fair margin, but their client service and return policies are exceptional. The Ritz Carlton hosts very nice facilities, but honestly for the cost, they are not materially better than many less expensive hotels. The difference is in service, and the way they make their patrons feel.

Ignore this fundamental truth, and none of these contents will matter. Embrace it, and you will succeed. The goal is to create Raving Fans at every opportunity. The clients you help will have friends and family getting married, and you want them to insist on you to handle them.

Your ultimate goal with every event is to create a Raving Fan. This is a client who is willing to give you a love letter (testimonial), act as a referral source, and, hire you again. We will address building your business and marketing later in the book, but there is absolutely no substitute for an enthusiastic endorsement from a client who has enjoyed your service.

We have structured this book to lead with items and information that apply to all or most events, with specific sections addressing unique aspects of a traditional events such as Bar mitzvahs.

Initial Consultation Interview

Stylistically this is your client's first impression. Dress impressively professional, and if you are not meeting in your own storefront or venue, set the meeting at a location reasonably befitting the purpose.

The client should do most of the talking. Listen. Seriously to what they want, what they worry about, and ask lots of open ended questions. Take detailed notes, and as you get your business established, bring a note taker, so you can focus on what is being said.

If you are meeting in your storefront, arrange for a light snack and beverages to be served in an environment that shows off your style in table dressing, and venue.

Get a sense of what they want from their wedding professional, and if they don't know, be in a position to intelligently explain options.

After the meeting follow up with a professional preferably hand written note expressing your joy in meeting the client expressing excitement for the opportunity to help with an important moment in their lives.

Consider bringing a portfolio (discussed below) for events you have handled in the past if meeting in a third party location. Have yours ready if meeting at the storefront.

Be mindful of the client's time and make sure this meeting doesn't take longer than an hour.

There is a substantial amount of information that should be collected in the initial consultation Including:

Names, phone numbers, addresses and emails for bride and groom

Event Specifications

Event Date

Event Venue if preference or already chosen

Event budget (ballpark)

Estimated Guest Count

Special and out of town guests

Seating arrangements or preferences

Preferred Menu – food and drink – dietary limitations

Level of Consultation – partial (month of, day of etc.) or full

Wedding Theme or Style if Any including preferred décor

Color Palette if selected

Type of ceremony – church, beach, hotel, outdoor, modern traditional, or unique

Comments on personal style – interests of the couple, special wedding requests, hobbies, military themes or celebration to be included

How to Build an Event Planner Portfolio

A huge part of any planner's business is helping the client to visualize what you can do for them. Storefront and venue displays can often be helpful here, and hotels rely heavily upon them, but for the planner there is no more important element than the portfolio.

As you plan magical weddings, sweet sixteen parties, or banquets, your portfolio will grow with different venues, themes, menus, and experiences. But what if you have never done a wedding before? How do you prepare your portfolio?

Keep in mind that a portfolio is there to help the bride and groom imagine the possibilities for their wedding. It is absolutely professional and appropriate to include representative photos of venues, plated food, and wedding themes, so long as you are able to deliver the vision depicted.

The notebook

The planner should have a very nice notebook, leather bound or otherwise (no grocery store binders), that can highlight aspects of every wedding. The notebook should be broken into Profile, Venue, Menu, Theme, and Packages

Profile: This is where you start. The most important thing you are selling is you. This section should include your credentials, background, relevant experience, and most of all references. These are testimonials from people who know you and will comment on your abilities, organizational skills, client service, and ability to deliver a fantastic wedding experience. This is where you begin to get the client excited about who they are hiring.

Venue: Many wedding planners aspire to have their own venue as business grows, and the best venues are designed with flexibility that allows for every theme of wedding from rustic, to vintage, and beyond. Most venues have well done photos that they will be glad to share with you for inclusion in your portfolio. As you gain experience, be sure to have the photographer take photos that reflect your vision, so you can build your own book of work. Be sure to have a variety of locations with various capacities, and in different price ranges to serve your clients. Check pricing regularly or have the venues advise you of pricing changes to avoid surprises.

Menus: Nothing sells a catering menu like attractive photographs of the food properly plated. Linens, and other details are important as well, but it is perfectly reasonable to reach out to local caterers and request professional photos of their catered offerings for your portfolio. If the menu is to be served buffet style, the caterer should provide photos of the food and equipment. You want to ensure that your caterer shows up with a menu and serving items befitting the professionalism called for by your event. Be sure to have a variety of offerings to suit all events.

Theme: Until you have well done photos documenting your wedding theme options, you will have to be creative here. Local party rental stores have a number of items that can be rented as centerpieces and decorations to assist with wedding themes, and photos of these items well staged can help you customers imagine the theme options. This is also a great way to expand your business with additional sources of revenue as you build a brand. Get permission of the happy couples you work with and include their images. It will help new clients imagine their own perfect day.

Other: Some wedding planners like to provide their clients with checklists, or follow along planners of their own to keep up with wedding timelines and details. This is a matter of personal preference, and should only be done where some money has been paid by the client in advance. The danger in this offering is that a client will use your tools to try to handle this themselves.

How to Charge For Your Services

Hourly – These packages include a set number of hours driven by a budget agreed upon by the client. Planners' rates range from $75 to more than $150 per hour. Consulting packages typically billed by the hour consist of the client sitting down with the planner and asking questions based on the area or areas they need help in. This may be pulling together design ideas, confirming or suggesting vendor or venue choices or ensuring that the client is on track and has not forgotten anything. These types of meetings typically take place early in the planning process. These meetings are a great opportunity for the planner to upsell the client and recommend a Day of Coordination or even a Full Service wedding package. Luckily for you, many times the client will realize they really do need more help than they had originally thought. However, these recommendations should be reserved until after the session has completed, as the client is paying you for your expertise, not your sales pitch.

Daily – Some clients want to be more involved in the planning of their event, and hire a wedding or event planner to manage details on the day of the event. Charges for these events range from $1000 to $2000 dollars to manage the event for the day. Although this package is typically booked well in advance of the wedding, the wedding planner does not get involved until 1-2 weeks prior to wedding day.

As a day of coordinator, responsibilities include creating a detailed timeline, contacting the vendors for formal introductions, confirming day of contact information and reviewing copies of all contracts to clarify all contractual obligations of all vendors. After discussing the client's vision the planner would be in charge of running the event. And on the day of the event the planner's responsibilities would be to be present at the venue and ensure every detail is set up the way the client has envisioned it.

As a Day-Of Coordinator, you should also be the liaison between the client and the vendors for the day. This greatly relieves the bride, for example from unnecessary stress, which is, in a nutshell what being a planner really is about. During the event, the planner's responsibility is to ensure everything runs smoothly. The goal is to adhere to the timeline, but in the event that this isn't possible it is the planner's responsibility to ensure that events are rearranged in such a way that incurs minimal cost and stress to the client, their families and their guests.

The package cost for Day of Coordination can vary widely depending on the area of the country, the size of the wedding and if there are one or two locations.

Full-service planners range from $3,000 to more than **$10,000**, depending on experience and demand. In some instances these are flat fee engagements, and in others the fee is a percentage of the total wedding cost ranging from 10-20%. Many planners who are well-established will only do full service since this gives them full control of the look and feel of the event upon which their name, and thereby brand depend.

In this package, the planner is practically running the show from conception to execution. Full service planners recommend the vendors, which gives them the opportunity to work with vendors they are familiar with and can trust. They also typically are very involved with the planning of the décor, flowers, linens, rentals and printed materials. They also take care of all of the details included in the Day of Coordination package.

Percentage Contingent Agreement

CLIENT-PLANNER AGREEMENT

This Client-Planner Agreement entered into this_____day of _____ by and between
_____ ("Planner") and_____Client.

Client desires to engage planner to perform event planning services for a_____and said planner desires to perform these event planning services for the event on_____.

SECTION 1. SERVICES: Planner shall organize and co-ordinate all mutually agreed upon service as set forth in Addendum A. The forgoing shall be collectively known as services.

SECTION 2. COMPENSATION AND PAYMENT: The following fees shall apply.

2.1 Client shall pay planner 15% (fifteen) of the total event cost to provide the services referenced in Addendum A.

2.2 The total sum of all fees for each service provided as set forth in Addendum A.

2.3 Any additional charges plus planner's 15% (fifteen) for services requested by the client that is not included in the initial contract fee.

2.4 Reasonable and necessary lodging and travel expenses actually incurred. Upon receipt of an expense report with supporting documentation (invoices). No travel or lodging expense shall apply for events within a 25 (twenty five) mile radius of downtown

City_____State_____ all such expenses in excess of $50 (fifty) and travel plans must be approved in advance by the client.

2.5 $50% (fifty) of the total contract fee including services and planner's fee upon execution of this agreement. 25% (twenty five) 1 (one) month prior to the scheduled event. 25% (twenty five) 5 (five) days prior to the event.

2.6 Full contract fee shall be due and owing upon signing of this agreement.

SECTION 3: TERMINATIONS: The effective date here of shall be the date upon which the last party to the agreement signs the agreement. It shall remain in effect until all obligations under the agreement have been completed.

3.1 Either party to the agreement may terminate his (her) agreement with or without cause providing at least 60 (Sixty) days written notice to the other party. The planner will refund any client monies paid minus (-) cost and planner's fees already incurred.

3.2 CLIENT CANCELLATION: Within 60 (sixty) days of the event are subject to full planner's fee, charges up to the date of the cancellation in addition to any cost incurred.

3.3 PLANNER CANCELLATION: Within 60 (sixty) days of the event are subject to full client refund of monies paid Minus (-) non-refundable deposits or charges.

SECTION 4: CONTRACTS SIGNING: Planner shall not enter into any contracts on behalf of the client. The planner will provide the client with information including costs, contracts, and service provisions for potential service providers. The client will establish all necessary contracts within the time frame as set forth by the desired service provider.

SECTION 5: INDEMNIFY (Secure against hurt). Except as otherwise prohibited by law each party shall indemnify and hold the other party harmless from all claims, actions, suits, losses, and expenses of any nature for its employees or subcontractors, breach of their agreement, negligence or intentional misconduct.

SECTION 6: GOVERNING LAWS AND VENUE: This agreement shall be governed by the laws of the state of _____ (Your Company's home state). Client and planner consent and agree that any legal action or proceedings arising hereunder shall be brought there.

SECTION 7: NOTICES: All notices, modifications, demands, requests or other communications given pursuant to this agreement shall be given in writing and shall be deemed to have been given if delivered by hand, facsimile or certified mail, effective upon receipt of such notice, demand, request or other communication and signature by both parties.

The Client and Planner each cause this Agreement to be executed in their respective names. All as of the last date written below:

SMITH'S EVENT

CLIENT   PLANNER
SIGNATURE_____   SIGNATURE_____

NAME_____   NAME _____

Hourly Rate Agreement

CLIENT-PLANNER AGREEMENT

This Client-Planner Agreement entered into this_____day of _____ by and between
_____ ("Planner") and_____Client.

Client desires to engage planner to perform event planning services for a_____and said planner desires to perform these event planning services for the event on_____.

SECTION 1. SERVICES: Planner shall organize and co-ordinate all mutually agreed upon service as set forth in Addendum A. The forgoing shall be collectively known as services.

SECTION 2. COMPENSATION AND PAYMENT: The following fees shall apply.

2.1 Client shall pay planner an hourly rate of _____ to provide the services referenced in Addendum A.

2.2 The total sum of all fees for each service provided as set forth in Addendum A.

2.3 Any additional charges plus planner's 15% (fifteen) for services requested by the client that is not included in the initial contract fee.

2.4 Reasonable and necessary lodging and travel expenses actually incurred. Upon receipt of an expense report with supporting documentation (invoices). No travel or lodging expense shall apply for events within a 25 (twenty five) mile radius of downtown

City_____State_____ all such expenses in excess of $50 (fifty) and travel plans must be approved in advance by the client.

2.5 $50% (fifty) of the total contract fee including services and planner's fee upon execution of this agreement. 25% (twenty five) 1 (one) month prior to the scheduled event. 25% (twenty five) 5 (five) days prior to the event.

2.6 Full contract fee shall be due and owing upon signing of this agreement.

SECTION 3: TERMINATIONS: The effective date here of shall be the date upon which the last party to the agreement signs the agreement. It shall remain in effect until all obligations under the agreement have been completed.

3.1 Either party to the agreement may terminate his (her) agreement with or without cause providing at least 60 (Sixty) days written notice to the other party. The planner will refund any client monies paid minus (-) cost and planner's fees already incurred.

3.2 CLIENT CANCELLATION: Within 60 (sixty) days of the event are subject to full planner's fee, charges up to the date of the cancellation in addition to any cost incurred.

3.3 PLANNER CANCELLATION: Within 60 (sixty) days of the event are subject to full client refund of monies paid Minus (-) non-refundable deposits or charges.

SECTION 4: CONTRACTS SIGNING: Planner shall not enter into any contracts on behalf of the client. The planner will provide the client with information including costs, contracts, and service provisions for potential service providers. The client will establish all necessary contracts within the time frame as set forth by the desired service provider.

SECTION 5: INDEMNIFY (Secure against hurt). Except as otherwise prohibited by law each party shall indemnify and hold the other party harmless from all claims, actions, suits, losses, and expenses of any nature for its employees or subcontractors, breach of their agreement, negligence or intentional misconduct.

SECTION 6: GOVERNING LAWS AND VENUE: This agreement shall be governed by the laws of the state of _____ (Your Company's home state). Client and planner consent and agree that any legal action or proceedings arising hereunder shall be brought there.

SECTION 7: NOTICES: All notices, modifications, demands, requests or other communications given pursuant to this agreement shall be given in writing and shall be deemed to have been given if delivered by hand, facsimile or certified mail, effective upon receipt of such notice, demand, request or other communication and signature by both parties.

The Client and Planner each cause this Agreement to be executed in their respective names. All as of the last date written below:

SMITH'S EVENT

CLIENT   PLANNER
SIGNATURE_____   SIGNATURE_____

NAME_____   NAME _____

Flat Fee Agreement

CLIENT-PLANNER AGREEMENT

This Client-Planner Agreement entered into this_____day of
_____ by and between
_____ ("Planner") and_____Client.

Client desires to engage planner to perform event planning services
for a_____and said planner desires to perform these event
planning services for the event on_____.

SECTION 1. SERVICES: Planner shall organize and co-ordinate all
mutually agreed upon service as set forth in Addendum A. The
forgoing shall be collectively known as services.

SECTION 2. COMPENSATION AND PAYMENT: The following fees shall
apply .

2.1 Client shall pay planner a flat fee in the amount of _____ to
provide the services referenced in Addendum A.

2.2 The total sum of all fees for each service provided as set forth in
Addendum A.

2.3 Any additional charges plus planner's 15% (fifteen) for services
requested by the client that is not included in the initial contract
fee.

2.4 Reasonable and necessary lodging and travel expenses actually
incurred. Upon receipt of an expense report with supporting
documentation (invoices). No travel or lodging expense shall apply
for events within a 25 (twenty five) mile radius of downtown

City_____State_____ all such expenses in
excess of $50 (fifty) and travel plans must be approved in advance
by the client.

2.5 $50% (fifty) of the total contract fee including services and planner's fee upon execution of this agreement. 25% (twenty five) 1 (one) month prior to the scheduled event. 25% (twenty five) 5 (five) days prior to the event.

2.6 Full contract fee shall be due and owing upon signing of this agreement.

SECTION 3: TERMINATIONS: The effective date hereof shall be the date upon which the last party to the agreement signs the agreement. It shall remain in effect until all obligations under the agreement have been completed.

3.1 Either party to the agreement may terminate his (her) agreement with or without cause providing at least 60 (Sixty) days written notice to the other party. The planner will refund any client monies paid minus (-) cost and planner's fees already incurred.

3.2 CLIENT CANCELLATION: Within 60 (sixty) days of the event are subject to full planner's fee, charges up to the date of the cancellation in addition to any cost incurred.

3.3 PLANNER CANCELLATION: Within 60 (sixty) days of the event are subject to full client refund of monies paid Minus (-) non-refundable deposits or charges.

SECTION 4: CONTRACTS SIGNING: Planner shall not enter into any contracts on behalf of the client. The planner will provide the client with information including costs, contracts, and service provisions for potential service providers. The client will establish all necessary contracts within the time frame as set forth by the desired service provider.

SECTION 5: INDEMNIFY (Secure against hurt). Except as otherwise prohibited by law each party shall indemnify and hold the other party harmless from all claims, actions, suits, losses, and expenses of any nature for its employees or subcontractors, breach of their agreement, negligence or intentional misconduct.

SECTION 6: GOVERNING LAWS AND VENUE: This agreement shall be governed by the laws of the state of _____ (Your Company's home state). Client and planner consent and agree that any legal action or proceedings arising hereunder shall be brought there.

 SECTION 7: NOTICES: All notices, modifications, demands, requests or other communications given pursuant to this agreement shall be given in writing and shall be deemed to have been given if delivered by hand, facsimile or certified mail, effective upon receipt of such notice, demand, request or other communication and signature by both parties.

The Client and Planner each cause this Agreement to be executed in their respective names. All as of the last date written below:

SMITH'S EVENT

CLIENT   PLANNER
SIGNATURE_____   SIGNATURE_____

NAME_____   NAME _____

Venue Checklist

This checklist is to be used for interviewing venues, and tracking their answers to insure that they are a good fit for the client's needs. While weddings are most often contemplated with venue planning, this checklist should serve very well very every kind of event. It is always a good idea to tour the venue early where economics permit, to see for yourself if the place is as nice as the well situated online pictures make it appear to be. When a venue impresses you, be sure to document that, and keep it mind. Relationships with quality reliable vendors are absolutely essential to success in this business.

Capacity

____	Reception Area
____	Theatre/Meeting Room
____	Dining Area

Caterer

____	Exclusive caterers?
____	In-house tables/linens/chairs? If so, check out the quality.
____	Typical menu cost per head for cocktails, heavy appetizers, etc.
____	Bar tender charges?
____	Serving Charges?
____	Cake cutting charges?
____	Minimum food and beverage spend?
____	How early can your caterer arrive day of event to set up?

Rental Fees

_____ Usually negotiable, especially for a major brand/off day
_____ Does fee include a set up day?
_____ How early/late can your teams load in?
_____ Any discount for payment by check or early payment?
_____ Hotels should waive any room rentals when F&B meets a min.

Bathrooms

_____ Will you need to provide extra amenities to make the room nicer
_____ Cleanliness – poorly kept restrooms reflect poorly managed venue
_____ Number of stalls vs. number of guests

Parking

_____ Existent?
_____ Fee to use parking lot?
_____ Valets – included? Is there a preferred valet company?
_____ Buses – if using buses - is there room to turn around, unload?

Shipments

_____ Will the venue accept and store boxes a few days before event? $?

Audiovisual Team

_____ Exclusive AV Company?

____ What tech operators are included, if any? (lighting tech, sound,   camera)
____ Cost of in-house AV Team/hour/operator
____ What AV exists in house? See the quality of the projector and check compatibility.
____ Internet Access- speed and logistics (do you need to drop lines, $$$)
____ Cost to use existing Internet lines

Stages

____ Note any restrictions and size dimensions
____ Height from ground to hang points
____ See stage lighting with the room dark
____ Existing backdrops, can you utilize these for event?
____ If a stage must be brought in understand load-in logistics/restrictions

Registration/Place card area

____ Is there a clean, open space near entrance of venue and in front of main room?
____ How much signage can be placed outside of meeting room, in common areas?
____ Will other events be held during meeting/wedding/party?
____ Does venue have staff to help with registration/guiding guests to room?

Entrance

____ Opportunity to brand/decorate entrance area?
____ Curb appeal; are you comfortable with the current look/feel of the entrance?

Reception Area

    _____ How close is the area to the ceremony/meeting room?

    _____ Ideally a large open space with the ability to brand/decorate

    _____ What furniture can be utilized for event?

    _____ Will venue take away existing furniture you don't want for your   event?

Any charges?

    _____ How early can you set up in this area?

Other Clients

    _____ Who else has held events at this venue in recent months?

    _____ Testimonials? Can you contact references?

    _____ Has a major competitor hosted parties at this venue for a similar client base?

Electronic versions of this tool with room for notes are available upon request at **products@newbizplaybook.com**.

Marketing for Event Planners

Of all the challenges a new event planner faces, marketing the business can feel the most overwhelming. The good news is that you can very easily, and inexpensively market your business to a receptive target audience. The challenge will be follow through and consistency in maintaining exposure for your brand.

Whole books have been written on the subject of marketing, and this material is not designed to replace them. Our hope is to provide you with guidance as to how to spend your time, and where. You should understand the pros and cons of the various options out there, to make intelligent decisions on your ROI or return on investment. Everyone has different results with different media. As important as this is to your success, you should track where your leads (especially the ones that hire you), are coming from. Advertising that appears expensive at the outset, maybe cheap relative to other options when you see the revenue it is generating.

Website/SEO

Your website if properly done can be a very useful marketing tool, and may be one of the places you spend early money, once you start getting gigs. Wordpress.org, has some incredibly easy templated websites that can get you started. If you can get to a place where you are on the first or second page of google with your site, which is very doable, this will be the single most effective marketing vehicle you have. Keep in mind, you aren't looking to be first when someone types "wedding planner." You are looking to be first when someone type "wedding planner in Cleveland." The difference between these two is what makes it vastly easier to rise to the top. I have, with no training whatsoever, been able to get several service based websites on the first page of google.

The key is to duplicate the search you want to be relevant for. For example, if the hope is that you come up first when someone types "event planners in St. Louis," do that search, and then go to the sites on the first page and a half of google, and look at the content. You are specifically looking for whether there are videos or pictures, how often your key search term appears.

You are also looking for the titles used for the website's pages. For example if you click on a page, at the top right side of that page there will be a tab, with some language on it that is designed to summarize the content of that page. These are title tags, and this research on content, will tell you what you need to emulate to get to the top of google. Be careful. Copying text and directly duplicating material, or over using a few key words will get you punted from key word searches, which would kill the effectiveness of your website. When you start to book events, you should consider early investment in a great website with an SEO (search engine optimization) professional to help you.

We recommend that at a minimum, a third of all profits go back into the business to grow it and help with important investments in the business. This investment would be at the top of that list. If you have some resources already saved, this would boost visibility substantially and increase the speed with which your business gets noticed. There are a number of free-lance website development options out there. Do your research as this is a hugely important investment.

Networking and Word of Mouth

Experienced, successful event planners will tell you that most of their new business comes from referrals and relationships they have formed with clients, and others in the business such as wedding photographers, and other wedding service providers. The challenge is to reach the level where the "machine" is sending you leads on a constant basis. As you build relationships with these professionals, and help them to build their businesses, it is reasonable to expect that they help with yours. You should be candid in hiring these folks about what you are looking for. It is reasonable to demand promptness, professionalism, responsiveness, and elite service from these folks. Let them know that in your mind they are an extension of your brand, and if they provide an exceptional experience for your bride, you will help build their businesses. It is interesting to hear from new planners that they feel uncomfortable asking these folks for referrals. That is part of the job here

In the beginning you should be very vocal to your personal network of friends and family to let them know you have begun to do this work, being sure to emphasize all of your efforts, research, and time spent getting to know the business.

Wedding Shows

Wedding and Bridal Shows – Few venues will give you as much exposure to potential clients in such a short amount of time as Wedding shows. They are also among the most expensive marketing options available to a new startup. Prices for large city shows range from $1000 for a small booth to more than $1600 for a larger one. These costs don't include expenses for any attention getting show pieces you may want to feature. There will also be some competition among other planners vying for the business of the same clients in a relatively small setting. – Tip If you are just starting out, and don't have a good portfolio of pictures of your work (which we will talk about getting inexpensively or free from photographers later), research designs you like online with sites like Pinterest and others and create a book of "ideas we love for your weeding." Make sure these are things that you will be able to recreate with reasonable effort if asked to do so, but visualization is very important to getting clients to hire you.

Social Media

Social media is an incredibly effective and inexpensive means of advertising your business, and to a limited degree it is worth your time to learn how to get your brand up and running on Facebook, Instagram, twitter, Pinterest, and snapchat. This is how you build a following, and stay relevant to others who need to think of you first when they or someone they know decides to get married. In the beginning these are free if not very inexpensive. Once you get traction, placing ads may make a huge difference. Next to Wedding Shows, this can be the most impactful marketing media available to you.

Ratings and specialty sites

There are a number of sites like Yelp, which allow businesses to put up very basic profiles for free. In the beginning, it can be helpful to put your site and business on as many of these as possible so that these sites point back to your website and business. When you sign up, you will be pitched on pay packages that help boost your chances of appearing early on these sites. In our experience these types of investment don't generate nearly as many live leads as search engine optimization. It is important to monitor these sites, and to regularly search for your site so that you can see what reviews are out there both good and bad, which could impact your business.

Phone books, mailers and other print advertising

We address these last, because frankly they are not very effective in generating revenue relative to the cost, at least in this business. At some point, you may be large enough to require a better add in a phone book, or need to have mail outs for clients to stay in front of them, but getting email addresses, and electronic communication is vastly more effective. We simply don't recommend spending startup dollars here.

You may have need for printed material in the form of business cards or trifolds, which can be handed out to guests who visit you at wedding shows etc. These are necessary expenditures, and when they are printed it should be high quality work on good card or paper stock. This stuff represents your brand, which must be elite if you want to command larger fees with your engagements.

We have included a great example of a tri fold in word form, so you don't have to play with formatting or make one yourself. Simply cut and paste photos or logos and add content as you see fit. Below is a printed example with two sides of a suggested layout, with content references that will allow you adjust the tri-fold to fit your business.

Food and Beverage Planning

Appetizers

As you determine the appetizer quantity, consider what purpose the appetizers will serve. If you're serving appetizers before a main meal, you don't need as many as you do if the appetizers are the meal itself. Because appetizers are different from other food items, how much you need depends on several factors. Appetizers don't lend themselves to a quantity chart, per se, but let the following list guide you:

- For appetizers preceding a full meal, you should have at least four different types of appetizers and six to eight pieces (total) per person. For example, say you have 20 guests. In that case, you'd need at least 120 total appetizer pieces.

- For appetizers without a meal, you should have at least six different types of appetizers. You should also have 12 to 15 pieces (total) per person. For example, if you have 20 guests, you need at least 240 total appetizer pieces. This estimate is for a three-hour party. Longer parties require more appetizers.

- The more variety you have, the smaller portion size each type of appetizer will need to have. Therefore, you don't need to make as much of any one particular appetizer.

- When you serve appetizers to a crowd, always include bulk-type appetizers. Bulk-type foods are items that aren't individually made, such as dips or spreads. If you forgo the dips and spreads, you'll end up making hundreds of individual appetizer items, which may push you over the edge. To calculate bulk items, assume 1 ounce equals 1 piece.

- Always try to have extra items, such as black and green olives and nuts, for extra filler.

When appetizers precede the meal, you should serve dinner within an hour. If more than an hour will pass before the meal, then you need to increase the number of appetizers. Once again, always err on the side of having too much rather than too little.

Quantity planning for soups, sides, main courses, and desserts

The following tables can help you determine how much food you need for some typical soups, sides, main courses, and desserts. If the item you're serving isn't listed here, you can probably find an item in the same food group to guide you.

You may notice a bit of a discrepancy between the serving per person and the crowd servings. The per-person serving is based on a plated affair (where someone else has placed the food on the plates and the plates are served to the guests). In contrast, buffet-style affairs typically figure at a lower serving per person because buffets typically feature more side dish items than a plated meal does. Don't use the quantity tables as an exact science; use them to guide you and help you make decisions for your particular crowd. If you're serving a dish that you know everyone loves, then make more than the table suggests. If you have a dish that isn't as popular, you can get by with less.

Soups and Stews

Soup or Stew	Per Person	Crowd of 25	Crowd of 50
Served as a first course	1 cup	5 quarts	2-1/2 gallons
Served as an entree	1-1/2 to 2 cups	2 to 2-1/2 gallons	4 gallons

Main Courses

Entree	Per Person	Crowd of 25	Crowd of 50
Baby-back ribs, pork spareribs, beef short ribs	1 pound	25 pounds	50 pounds
Casserole	N/A	Two or three 9-x-13-inch casseroles	Four or five 9-x-13-inch casseroles
Chicken, turkey, or duck (boneless)	1/2 pound	13 pounds	25 pounds
Chicken or turkey (with bones)	3/4 to 1 pound	19 pounds	38 pounds
Chili, stew, stroganoff, and other chopped meats	5 to 6 ounces	8 pounds	15 pounds

Ground beef	1/2 pound	13 pounds	25 pounds
Maine lobster (about 2 lbs. each)	1	25	50
Oysters, clams, and mussels (medium to large)	6 to 10 pieces	100 to 160 pieces	200 to 260 pieces
Pasta	4 to 5 ounces	7 pounds	16 pounds
Pork	14 ounces	22 pounds	44 pounds
Roast (with bone)	14 to 16 ounces	22 to 25 pounds	47 to 50 pounds
Roast cuts (boneless)	1/2 pound	13 pounds	25 pounds
Shrimp (large: 16 to 20 per pound)	5 to 7 shrimp	7 pounds	14 pounds
Steak cuts (T-bone, porterhouse, rib-eye)	16 to 24 ounces	16 to 24 ounces per person	16 to 24 ounces per person
Turkey (whole)	1 pound	25 pounds	50 pounds

Side Dishes

Side Dish	Per Person	Crowd of 25	Crowd of 50
Asparagus, carrots, cauliflower, broccoli, green beans, corn kernels, peas, black-eyed peas, and so on	3 to 4 ounces	4 pounds	8 pounds
Corn on the cob (broken in halves when serving buffet-style)	1 ear	20 ears	45 ears
Pasta (cooked)	2 to 3 ounces	3-1/2 pounds	7 pounds
Potatoes and yams	1 (medium)	6 pounds	12 pounds
Rice and grains (cooked)	1-1/2 ounces	2-1/2 pounds	5 pounds

Side Salads

Ingredient	Per Person	Crowd of 25	Crowd of 50
Croutons (medium size)	N/A	2 cups	4 cups
Dressing (served on the side)	N/A	4 cups	8 cups
Fruit salad	N/A	3 quarts	6 quarts
Lettuce (iceberg	N/A	4 heads	8 heads

or romaine)

Lettuce (butter or red leaf)	N/A	6 heads	12 heads
Potato or macaroni salad	N/A	8 pounds	16 pounds
Shredded cabbage for coleslaw	N/A	6 to 8 cups (about 1 large head of cabbage)	12 to 16 cups (about 2 large heads of cabbage)
Vegetables (such as tomato and cucumber)	N/A	3 cups	6 cups

Breads

Bread	Per Person	Crowd of 25	Crowd of 50
Croissants or muffins	1-1/2 per person	3-1/2 dozen	7 dozen
Dinner rolls	1-1/2 per person	3-1/2 dozen	7 dozen
French or Italian bread	N/A	Two 18-inch loaves	Four 18-inch loaves

Desserts

Dessert	Per Person	Crowd of 25	Crowd of 50
Brownies or bars	1 to 2 per person	2-1/2 to 3 dozen	5-1/2 to 6 dozen
Cheesecake	2-inch wedge	Two 9-inch cheesecakes	Four 9-inch cheesecakes
Cobbler	1 cup	Two 9-x-9-x-2-inch pans	Four 9-x-9-x-2-inch pans
Cookies	2 to 3	3 to 4 dozen	6 to 8 dozen
Ice cream or sorbet	8 ounces	1 gallon	2 gallons
Layered cake or angel food cake	1 slice	Two 8-inch cakes	Four 8-inch cakes
Pie	3-inch wedge	Two or three 9-inch pies	Four or five 9-inch pies
Pudding, trifles, custards, and the like	1 cup	1 gallon	2 gallons
Sheet cake	2-x-2-inch piece	1/4 sheet cake	1/2 sheet cake

Alcohol and Beverage Planning

Concerning drinks, let the following list guide you:

Soft drinks: One to two 8-ounce servings per person per hour.

Punch: One to two 4-ounce servings per person per hour.

Tea: One to two 8-ounce servings per person per hour.

Coffee: One to two 4-ounce servings per person per hour.

Water: Always provide it. Two standard serving pitchers per table are usually enough.

Again, err on the side of having too much. If people are eating a lot and having fun, they tend to consume more liquid.

Alcohol Consumption and Pricing Projection Tool

There is always some subjectivity in alcohol planning. The assumption here is that 75% of the guests are drinking alcohol. This should be discussed, as a higher percentage of children in attendance, a group of heavier drinkers etc., could impact these assumptions.

As always we recommend adding 10% to all estimates. You will frustrate guests if there is insufficient alcohol, so make sure they are in agreement with your assumptions on numbers. They will know their guests better than anyone. The cost estimates assume average costs on beer, wine, and liquor. Premium beer, wine, and liquor would also mean increased costs. This also assumes equal consumption i.e. 25% each of beer, wine, and liquor. Beer drinkers tend to range closer to 40%, but these figures make scaling for your needs much easier.

The following should help plan for reception alcohol consumption. BD = beer drinker, WD = wine drinker, LD = liquor drinker

Small Wedding (100 guests)		
	Amount	Cost
Beer	5 cases per 25 BD	75.00
Wine	20 bottles per 25 WD	160.00
Liquor	6 750 ml bottles per 25 LD	90.00

Medium Wedding (200 guests)		
	Amount	Cost
Beer	9 cases per 50 BD	135.00
Wine	40 bottles per 50 WD	320.00
Liquor	12 750 ml bottles per 50 LD	180.00

Large Wedding (100)		
	Amount	Cost
Beer	3 Kegs 100 BD	270.00
Wine	79 bottles per 100 WD	632.00
Liquor	24 750 ml bottles per 100 LD	360.00

Linen Planning Tool

TABLE SIZE	SEATS	54" Sq	80" Sq	90" Sq	72x120"	70x170"	90x132"	90x156"	96" Rnd	108" Rnd	120" Rnd	126" Rnd	132" Rnd
4'x3'	4	Overlay	16x25" Drop										
6'x3'	6-8			Overlay	24x21" Drop	Box	To Floor All Sides						
8'x3'	8-10			Overlay	12x21" Drop	Box		To Floor All Sides	Overlay, Pinned	Overlay, Pinned	Overlay, Pinned		
6'x18"	3 (One Side)				26x27" Drop	Box			Overlay, Pinned	Overlay, Pinned	Overlay, Pinned		
8'x18"	4 (One Side)				18x27" Drop	Box							
30"x30"	4	12" Drop*	25" Drop*	To Floor All Sides									

Linen Planning Tool

TABLE SIZE	SEATS	54" Sq	80" Sq	90" Sq	72x120"	70x170"	90x132"	90x156"	96" Rnd	108" Rnd	120" Rnd	126" Rnd	132" Rnd
30" Round	3	Overlay 12 Drop*											
3 Round	4	Overlay 9" Drop	Overlay 22" Drop*						To Floor				
Café Table	Standing	Overlay 9" Drop	Overlay 22" Drop*	Overlay 27" Drop					Overlay 30" Drop		To Floor		
4 Round	6	Overlay Top	Overlay 16" Drop*	Overlay 21" Drop					Overlay 24" Drop	To Floor			
5 Round	8-10		Overlay 10" Drop*	Overlay 18" Drop					Overlay 18" Drop	Overlay 24" Drop	To Floor		
5½ Round	9-10		Overlay 7" Drop*	Overlay 12" Drop					Overlay 15" Drop	Overlay 21" Drop	27" Drop	To Floor	
6 Round	10-12		Overlay Top	Overlay 9" Drop					Overlay 12" Drop	Overlay 18" Drop	Overlay 24" Drop	27" Drop	To Floor
72 Round											1 Cloth Folded		
Serpentine	Buffet	3 Cloths with 2 Skirts			1 Cloth with 2 Skirts	1 Cloth							

Seating Planning Tool

Banquet Table

Table Size	Seating Capacity	Linen Size	Space Needed
6'	6-8	90" x 132"	11" x 7"
8'	8-10	90" x 156"	13' x 7'
Classroom 6'	4	70" x 170"	11' x 6'
Classroom 8'	6	70" x 170"	13' x 6'

Round Table

Table Size	Seating Capacity	Linen Size	Space Needed
2.5'	2-4	96" round	7' diameter
3'	4-5	96" round	8' diameter
4'	6-8	108" round	9' diameter
5'	8-10	120" round	10' diameter
6'	10-12	132" round	11' diameter

Cocktail Table

Table Size	Seating Capacity	Linen Size	Space Needed
2.5'	2-4	108" round	7' diameter
3'	4-5	120" round	8' diameter

Dance Floor Planning Tool

This tool has been designed to allow you to plan and scale necessary floor space for dancing. For parties greater than 250, simply use multiples of the tables below. If more than 50% of guests are expected to be dancing, ignore the guests invited column, and plan based upon the number of dancers in the second column.

Total Guests	Dancers	Dance FL Size	Floor SQ Feet
24	12	8'x8'	64
36	18	8'x12'	96
48	24	8'x16'	128
64	32	12'x12'	144
72	36	12'x16'	192
90	45	12'x20	240
96	48	16'x16'	256
120	60	16'x24'	384
128	64	16'x24'	384
144	72	16'x24'	384
150	75	20'x20'	400
168	84	16'x28'	448
180	90	20'x24'	480
192	96	16'x32'	512
210	105	20'x28'	560
250	125	24'x28'	672

Invoice Template

Your invoice is as much a reflection of your brand as any business card. You want to finish your engagement as professionally as you started it. We have included a template, and an electronic copy is available at **products@newbizplaybook.com**. Your invoice should include all of the following:

[Company Name]
[Company slogan]

INVOICE

[Street Address]
[City, ST ZIP Code]
Phone [Phone] | Fax [Fax]
[Email] | [Website]

INVOICE # [Invoice No.]
DATE [Date]

TO
[Name]
[Company Name]
[Street Address]
[City, ST ZIP Code]
Phone [Phone] | [Email]

FOR [Project or service description]
P.O. # [P.O. #]

Description	Amount

Total

Make all checks payable to [Company Name]
Payment is due within 30 days.
If you have any questions concerning this invoice, contact [Name] | [Phone] | [Email]

THANK YOU FOR YOUR BUSINESS!

Photographer Interview Questions

Attached are some questions to ask when interviewing photographers, but prior to that, you should speak to your client about what they want in terms of wedding photography both in the deliverable, and with the style of photographer and his interaction with guests, and the wedding party. The photographer should be willing to answer these questions and this interview will give you a sense of his or her business temperament. Eventually you will have a stable of talented vendors who can help you here based on your specific needs, and you may develop special requests that help you make the events you handle unique. *You should also be prepared to provide the photographer with any needed information such as divorced guests, who do not wish to be photographed together etc.

1. Do you have my date available?

2. Do you have an online portfolio that I, and/or my client can review to get a sense of your style, and how recent is the material on it?

3. How far in advance do I need to book with you?

4. How long have you been in business/How many weddings have you shot?

5. Are there references you can offer from prior clients or planners? Note: This is the important question in the interview. Do not hire someone who cannot provide you this information, and call at least a couple of the references to compare their answers to your photographer's responses to these questions.

6. How would you describe your photography style (e.g. traditional, photojournalistic, and creative)?

7. How would you describe your approach to interacting with wedding party and guests, i.e. blending in, stirring the pot for creative photos, choreographing shots?

8. What type of equipment do you use?

9. Are you shooting in digital or film format or both?

10. Do you shoot in color and black & white?

11. Can I give you a list of specific shots we would like?

12. How will you (and your assistants) be dressed?

13. Is it okay if other people take photos while you're taking photos?

14. Have you ever shot at (wedding/reception venue)? If not, would you be willing to visit in advance to plan?

15. What time will you arrive at the site and for how long will you shoot?

16. If my event lasts longer than expected, will you stay? Is there an additional charge?

17. Can you put together a slideshow of the bride and groom with provided photos and/or a real time slide show for viewing at the reception?

18. What information do you need from me before the wedding day?

19. What is your rate, and how is ownership of the photos handled? Bride and groom may want to own the photos to copy and use as they see fit, and this may impact price.

20. Are you the photographer who will shoot my wedding? If not, who will shoot it, and can I see their work? If so, who will be assisting you and how?

21. What are your travel charges/requirements if any?

22. Are you photographing other events on the same day as this event?

23. What type of album designs do you offer? Do you provide any assistance in creating an album?

24. Do you provide retouching, color adjustment or other corrective services?

25. How long after the wedding will I get the proofs? Will they be viewable online? On a CD?

26. What is the ordering process?

27. How long after I order my photos/album will I get them?

28. Will you give me the negatives or the digital images, and is there a fee for that?

29. When will I receive a written contract?

30. What is your refund/cancellation policy? Do you have someone who covers your events in case of emergency or equipment failure?

Florist Interview Questions

1. Do you have my date available?

2. Do you have an online portfolio that I, and/or my client can review to get a sense of your style, and how recent is the material on it?

3. How far in advance do I need to book with you?

4. How long have you been in business/How many weddings have you handled?

5. Are there references you can offer from prior clients or planners? Note: This is the important question in the interview. Do not hire someone who cannot provide you this information, and call at least a couple of the references to compare their answers to your photographer's responses to these questions.

6. Given the size of this wedding, flower preference, color scheme, and venue specifics for church and reception, what would you propose? Note: Do not lead with your budget. Advise that you are open and want to see the proposal for a few different packages, so that you can compare costs.

7. What time will you arrive at the site and how long will it take you to set up?

8. Who will be managing the setup?

9. Are you providing flowers for other events on the same day as this event?

10. Any rental fees for vases or decorations the florist is providing?

11. Any additional labor charges, taxes, or other fee?

12. When will I receive a written contract?

13. What is your refund/cancellation policy? Do you have someone who covers your events in case of emergency? Note: It is common to require a 50% down payment.

Weddings

Wedding Theme Ideas

A great way to get a bride and groom excited about hiring you is to help with creative wedding theme ideas. Use your creative flair here to develop style but the following are very trendy:

Unplugged: simple wedding in a beautiful area with a cellphone check. Encourage your guests to enjoy the event and each other if only for a night

#: the opposite of the unplugged wedding, encourage your guests to document and celebrate your wedding as they see it, but only if they promise to share. A fun way to take advantage of technology to ensure no perfect moment is missed

Vintage: 30's to 50's style dress based upon personal preference with flattering black and white photography and venues or style pieces, such as vintage cars that take your clients and their guests back to a simpler time. Gatsby type themes are a popular variant here, and the music selection for these is next level!

Simple destination: Instead of a wedding with only a few guests and a massive travel budget, set your wedding locally at a beach, or mountain or desert prized for amazing views and natural splendor.

Rustic: Simple elegant style, with comfort foods, in an environment that focuses on the people above all. This theme can be done classy and inexpensively with a proper vision, and give guests a warm and welcome feel.

Seasonal: A beautifully colorful pumpkin patch, or the stark glitter of winter snow can create a wonderful wedding vibe. Others prefer rolled up pants at the beach with simple cotton dresses, but however you do it, seasonal beauty can inspire a wonderful wedding experience

Wedding Planning Checklist

This checklist is intended to be used both in the actual planning of the wedding and in the pre-engagement discussions that give rise to the scope of work to be agreed between the parties. It should be included as an attachment for Addendum A to the agreement to describe items to be handled by the planner.

Checklist

The following checklist is an ideal timetable. Couples who do not have as much time as shown should plan their wedding in much the same order, using the checklist as a guide. Be sure to check things off as they are completed.

Immediately after the engagement:

_____   Hire photographer.
_____   Get engagement photo taken.
_____   Prepare engagement analysis.
_____   Discuss a budget and the size and style of the wedding and determine who/which family will pay for various aspects of the wedding. Key decisions about number of guests, and scope should be discussed.

_____   Consider making lists of who must be invited, who should be invited, and who it would be nice to invite to help narrow the guest list.
_____   First pass at wedding party including ring and flower bearers
_____   Evaluate venues, and check availability if inside 18 months.
_____   Make arrangements for the music at the wedding and reception.
_____   Make all transportation arrangements to and from the wedding.
_____   Make arrangements for passports if needed
_____   Choose a wedding date and time.

_____ Create a binder to organize your thoughts, photos, worksheets, etc.

_____ Make initial contact with vendors and obtain references.

_____ Meet with clergy member; schedule pre-marital counseling.

_____ Reserve wedding and reception sites; make initial catering contacts.

_____ Consider color palettes and dress for parties at wedding.

_____ Register at local bridal registries.

Six months or more before:

_____ Finalize the guest list.

_____ Send out Save the Date cards.

_____ Reserve a block of hotel rooms for out-of-town guests.

_____ Choose wedding rings.

_____ Send engagement announcement to newspapers.

_____ Select and order wedding gown, leaving ample time for delivery and alterations. – See advice for wedding gowns below

_____ Look for alteration specialist (if some- one other than bridal shop).

_____ Finalize the attendants (bridesmaids and groomsmen). Choose and order bridesmaids dresses.

_____ Purchase invitations.

_____ Select one usher for every 50 guests.

_____ Schedule wedding cake design appointment. Get estimates. Book the date.

_____ Implement diet and exercise program.

_____ Plan beauty preparations by checking with your salon for how far in advance they book wedding parties.

_____ Finalize all honeymoon plans. If traveling outside the country, check on visas, passports and inoculations.

_____ Sign up for dance lessons. Talk to instructor about choreographing a special dance routine to "wow" guests.

_____ Book vendors, securing dates by putting down deposit.

Four months or more before:

_____ Confirm final details with the caterer.

_____ Order napkins and purchase any other items needed for the ceremony and reception. Check with the caterer to see what he/she includes.

_____ Order invitations (25 extra) and personal stationery or "Thank You" notes.

_____ Book engagement photo session with enough time to submit photos to local newspapers.

_____ Visit the photographer again to discuss specifics. Use the "Photography Worksheet."

_____ Get estimates and order flowers and floral arrangements for wedding and reception.

_____ Get estimates and order balloons, decorations and favors for wedding and reception.

_____ Book room for wedding night.

Three months or more before:

_____ Order wedding rings. Allow time for any final engraving.

_____ Order tuxedos for the groomsmen and fathers.

Two months or more before:

_____ Mail invitations (six weeks before the wedding; eight weeks to out-of-town guests).

_____ Buy a wedding gift for future spouse and gifts for attendants and helpers.

_____ Finalize arrangements of accommodations for out-of-town attendants and guests.

One month or more before:

_____ Ready all accessories, shoes and lingerie for bridal gown.

_____ Have beauty consultant do a trial run with bride's hair and makeup. Schedule this appointment on the day the bridal portrait is taken and/or a party is planned or schedule on the day of your final dress fitting to see exactly how you will look on wedding day.

_____ Have final fitting for bridal gown and bridesmaids' dresses.

_____ Have bridal portrait taken.

_____ Have groomsmen registered and measured at the formal wear store.

_____ Check with the newspapers on wedding announcement requirements.

_____ Finalize plans for rehearsal dinner.

_____ Plan seating arrangements for the rehearsal dinner and reception.

_____ Review this checklist to be sure nothing has been missed.

_____ Complete change-of-address information for post-office.

_____ Keep current with "Thank You" notes for shower and early wedding gifts.

Two weeks before:

_____ Get the marriage license. Be sure to bring all needed documents.

_____ Inform or send rehearsal invitations including exact time and location to those who will attend the rehearsal and rehearsal dinner.

_____ Inquire about where bride, groom and attendants will dress for the ceremony.

_____ Review all details. Walk through the entire event considering things like parking, access for handicapped guests, etc.

_____ Confirm all transportation plans.

_____ Check in with caterer, photographer, videographer, musicians, DJ, florist, etc. to confirm all arrangements.

_____ "Break in" wedding shoes at home.

One week before:

_____ Appoint someone to act as an "organizer" to handle any last minute problems.
_____ Give a final guest count to the caterer.
_____ Review final details for those in the wedding party.
_____ Confirm honeymoon arrangements.
_____ Pack for the honeymoon.
_____ Enjoy a day with family and friends. Visit a day spa, have a massage, a facial and relax.

One day before:

_____ Attend the rehearsal and rehearsal dinner and give gifts to attendants.
_____ Give the rings and clergy's fee to the best man.
_____ Organize gown, accessories, etc. to go to ceremony.
_____ Get a manicure and pedicure.

On the wedding day:

_____ Mail wedding announcements.
_____ Get hair, makeup, etc. done.
_____ Enjoy the day!

Electronic versions of this tool with room for notes are available upon request at **products@newbizplaybook.com**

Wedding Budget Tool

In the attachments, we have included an excel spreadsheet complete with all formulas and entries needed for a great wedding budget tool. You can add items, or leave 0's in emails that don't apply. This tool will help you and your clients plan costs, and adjust in real time for increased costs or savings to allow the necessary flexibility.

The below is a print version you can complete as needed, electronic spreadsheet available at products@newbizplaybook.com

Total Budgeted Amount	
Guest Headcount (you can change this to see the figures below adjust)	
Ceremony	
Gown & Alterations	
Veil & Headpiece	
Bride's Accessories (lingerie, shoes, gloves, etc.)	
Bride's Hair & Makeup	
Bridesmaids Hair	
Bridesmaids wraps & purses	
Groomens Ties	
Site Fee	
Ceremony AV	
Officiant's Fee	
License and copies (4 @ $15 each)	
Accessories (arch, runner, etc.)	
Hotel	
Valet or Parking	
Food & Services ($X/Guest)	
Beverages & Bartenders ($40.00/Guest)	
Wedding Cake	
Recpetion Set up fees/dance floor	
Tax & Tip on food	
Florals	
Bridal Bouquet	
Flowers For Bride's Attendants ($60/Bride Attendant)	
Flowers For Groom's Attendants ($25/Groom Attendant)	
Other florals for guests	
tax on flowers	

Reception Centerpieces & Decor ($80 each*12)	
Children	
Child Care	
TV Rental	
Children's Meals	
Entertainment	
Ceremony Musician	
Reception Band	
Photographer	
Videographer	
Guests	
Shuttle Rental ($150/first run, $100 additional)	
Bride & Groom's Hotel Rooms	
Attendant Gifts ($x/Attendant)	
Donation/Favors ($x/Guest)	
Welcome Baskets ($x ea.)	

Printed Materials	
Invitations (reply cards, calligraphy, postage, etc.)	
Other Stationery (programs, thank you notes)	
Menu cards	
Welcome Party Invites/Rehearsal Dinner Invites	
TOTAL:	

Festivities around Wedding:	
(often these are covered by a parent or a separate budget)	
Bridesmaids Brunch	
	Tax/Tip 28%
Groomsmen Golf Outing	
Food on course	
Welcome Party	
food	
Alcohol	

	Tax
Rehearsal Dinner	
food	
alcohol	
Reception hall rental	
equipment rental (margarita machines lights etc.)	
silverware rental/ linen costs/plate & crystal costs	
waitstaff/bartenders	
decorations	
fun photo booth etc.	
Tip/Tax	Tax/Tip 28%
Total Wedding Festivities:	

Electronic versions of all of these tools are available upon request at **products@newbizplaybook.com**.

Counseling on the Wedding Dress

In some ways brides tend to think of wedding dress shopping as an ordinary affair in which one arrives at the store, looks at a couple of gowns, and buys one in the way any other garment is purchased. This is not the case.

The reverse is also true that some brides think of wedding dress shopping as something that ought to happen with ten of her closest friends and family. This is not the case.

As a wedding planner, this is an area where you may need to give unsolicited counsel. Your bride should know that it often takes 4-6 months to make a wedding dress, so anything custom made should be ordered well in advance. Eight to ten months before the wedding should allow ample time for production, and, if needed, alterations.

Similarly, the venue should be chosen before the dress is purchased as it may impact what is practical. An outdoor venue that could get muddy, and a long dress for example wouldn't make much sense.

Budgeting also can become an issue for brides who are not incorporating heirloom accessories from family etc. Costs of undergarments, shoes, jewelry and headpieces can be unwanted surprises that hammer your budget.

Wedding Tipping Conventions

A very common question wedding planners get is how to tip the various service providers and vendors that assist with the wedding. The following is a helpful starting point.

The Planner	If paid no tip is necessary. If not a $100-250 tip or personal gift is common.
Caterers	Check to see if gratuity is included in the arrangement. If not, $30-50 for servers and $125-250 for chefs and managers.
Photographer	For a great one $50-100 per shooter in addition to any purchases
Beauty	15-20% for stylists or $50-75 dollars if the stylist is a family friend who is not charging.
Musicians	20% of the bill or $50-75 per musician.
Officiant	$100-250 or charitable donation
Transportation	20% or $30-50 for hired drivers
Florist	10%
Videographer	Same as photographer
Tents	$40 per setup worker/attendant
Venue	See wait staff conventions

Reception Planner Contact Tool

Wedding Details

Wedding Date _____

Client Contact Name _____

Phone _____ email _____

Client Address _____

City _____ Zip _____

Wedding Venue Name _____

Rec Venue Name _____

Wedding Venue Address _____

City _____ Zip _____

Rec Venue Address _____

City _____ Zip _____

Photographer _____

Photographer Phone _____

Videographer _____

Videographer Phone _____

Caterer   _____

Caterer Phone   _____

Electronic versions of this spreadsheet are available upon request at products@newbizplaybook.com

Wedding Party Contact Tool

Bride & Groom_____   Flower Girl_____

Bride Parents _____   Ring Bearer_____

Groom Parents _____   Minister   _____

Made of Honor _____   Best Man   _____

Gparents Bride _____   Gparents Groom _____

Groom's Men	Brides Malds
1._____	1._____
2._____	2._____
3._____	3._____
4._____	4._____
5._____	5._____
6._____	6._____
7._____	7._____
8._____	8._____

Ushers

1._____   5._____

2._____   6._____

3._____   7._____

4._____   8._____

Events

Prayer/Grace _____   Toast Best Man _____

Father Bride Toast _____   Father Groom Toast _____

Dad Daughter Dance (song) _____

Mom Groom Dance (song) _____

Bride and Groom 1st Dance _____

Wedding Party (song) _____

Cake   Cutting   (song)   _____

Bouquet Toss (song) _____

Garter (song) _____

Special Requests _____

Groom Comments _____
Bride Comments _____

Special Requests _____

DJ musical genre preference _____

DJ style preference (active vs. camouflage)

Order of Events (please number 1-15)

Introduction	Toast	Father Daughter
Blessing	First Dance	Mother Groom
Bouquet Toss	Last Dance	Cake Cutting
Garter Toss	Other	Other
Other	Other	Other

Dinner Music or Special Songs

1._____ 2._____

3._____ 4._____

5._____ 6._____

7._____ 8._____

9._____ 10._____

11._____ 12._____

Electronic versions of this spreadsheet are available upon request at **products@newbizplaybook.com**.

Guest List Management Tool

This tool is most easily used in spreadsheet form. An excel file tool is available at newbizplaybook.com. For those who want to download it.

With proper planning, a fair amount of information is needed on each guest including:

1. First and last name

2. Telephone number

3. Address and/or email address

4. Invitation sent

5. Confirmed for attending wedding/or not

6. Confirmed for attending pre-wedding dinner/or not – out of town guests for example

7. Wedding gift

8. Thank you letter sent

Download a great tool for helping the bride and groom keep track of attendance, and their responsibilities for thank you cards etc. This tool also helps the event planner to track and make adjustments for food, dance etc., in the event that more or fewer guests attend than expected. Electronic versions of this spreadsheet will be sent to readers upon request at **products@newbizplaybook.com**.

Important People Contact List

This tool is related, but different. Wedding and event planners need to have visibility, and to some degree information about the VIP guests. Whoever is hiring you to plan their event wants the people dearest to them to enjoy it as much as possible. For you to build that robust referral network that will grow your business, you need to see to these folks.

For the VIP guests, you will want to know:

1. Full name

2. Relationship to the client

3. Cell phone if assisting with arrangements

4. Flight information if planner will be assisting with transportation (arrivals departures etc.)

5. Hotel details

6. Notes if needed.

We have a spreadsheet tool that will help to track these issues at **products@newbizplaybook.com**.

Packing Planning Tool

As silly as it sounds, one of the most common "emergencies," that plague weddings and events is forgotten items, missing clothing, or lost guest books etc. We have a spreadsheet tool to track these issues at **products@newbizplaybook.com**.

General Items	Box Number	Location for Wedding	Goes home with...
Pre-Ceremony Bride			
Dress/Suit	freestanding	Hotel Room	Sara Smith
Headpeice	freestanding	Hotel Room	Sara Smith
Jewelry	freestanding	Hotel Room	Mrs. Bride's Mom
Ring	freestanding	Hotel Room	Bride
Shoes	freestanding	Hotel Room	Sara Smith
Suitcase	freestanding	Hotel Room	Sara Smith
Wedding Party Gifts	1	Parents House	Mrs. Groom's Mom
Pre-Ceremony Groom			
Tux	freestanding	Hotel Room	Joe Jones
Jewelry	freestanding	Hotel Room	Groom
Shoes	freestanding	Hotel Room	Joe Jones
Tie, cuff links, etc	freestanding	Hotel Room	Joe Jones
Ring	freestanding	Hotel Room	Groom
Suitcase	freestanding	Hotel Room	Mrs. Groom's Mom
Wedding Party Gifts	3	Parents House	Mrs. Groom's Mom
Ceremony			
Flowers	freestanding	B Parents House	Given to guests
Decorations	4	B Parents House	Given to guests
Wedding signs	freestanding	Parents House	Mrs. Bride's Mom
Pre-Reception Bride			
Rec Dress	freestanding	Hotel Room	Sara Smith
Jewelry	freestanding	Hotel Room	Bride
Shoes	freestanding	Hotel Room	Sara Smith
Reception			
Cake Cutter for guests	1	Parents House	Planner
Glue, Scissors, Pens,	1	Parents House	Planner
Escort Cards	2	B Parents House	Planner
Escort Card Board	freestanding	G Parents House	Planner
Guest book,	2	gParents House	Planner
Garters	2	Parents House	Planner
Cake Knife For Pictures	2	Parents House	Planner
Kids Table Kits	2	Parents House	Planner
Etc.			
CPR Paddles	1	Church/Venue	
Parking Lot Signs	freestanding	Venue	Planner
Sewing Kit	1	Church/Venue	Planner
Deodorant/ etc	1	Church/Venue	Planner
Hair pins/ supply	1	Church/Venue	Planner
Emergency Kit	1	Church/Venue	Planner
Step stool	freestanding	Church/Venue	Planner

Vendor Contact Planning Sheet

Vendor	Business Name	Contact Name	Contact Number	Payment Status
Photographer				
Minister/Rabi				
Bakery				
Bar Tenders				
Wait staff				
Caterer				
Videographer				
D.J.				
Flowers				

Vendor Commitment Sheet

Vendor	Commitment	Arrival Time	Notes -	Gets Meal -
Photographer	8 hours x2			
Minister/Rabi				
Bakery		2.pm		
Bar Tenders				
Wait staff				No
Caterer				
Videographer				
D.J.				
Flowers				

Week of Wedding Schedule Tool

Time	Event	Location	Responsible Organizer
3:30 PM	Bride and Bridesmaids Arrive,	Bride's Apt	Maiden of Honor
4:30 PM	Rehearsal	The Church	Couple, Wedding Party
5:00 PM	Set up for Rehearsal Dinner	Groom's Parents' House	Groom, Groom's Parents
5:00 PM	Caterer arrives; begins set-up	Groom's Parents' House	Caterer
5:30PM	Couple arrives	Groom's Parents' House	The Couple
6:00 PM	Guests arrive	Groom's Parents' House	Everyone
7:00 PM	Food served	Groom's Parents' House	Caterer
8:15 PM	Caterer packs up	Groom's Parents' House	Caterer
9:30 PM	Couple leaves	Groom's Parents' House	The Couple
10:00 PM	Clean-up	Groom's Parents' House	Groom's Parents & volunteers
Begin at 7:30 AM	*SEE DAY OF SPREADSHEET*		
10:00 AM	Post Wedding Brunch	Acme Restaurant	Best Man and Maiden of Honor

Proper organization insures that everyone knows where to be and when. In many instances, there may be a need to add or remove events, change times, locations, or even responsible organizer. This tool allows everyone to be on the same page. The responsible organizer examples above are not intended to be a comment as to who should traditionally handle what. They are only present as an example. Electronic versions of this spreadsheet are available upon request at **products@newbizplaybook.com**.

Day of Wedding Schedule Tool

When	What	Where	Who
	Pre-Ceremony		
7:00 AM	Bride wakes up	Bride's Apt	Bride
7:30 AM	Friends arrive to do hair & makeup	Bride's Apt	Bride + friends
8:00 AM	pick up decorations	Wedding Planner Storage	Wedding Stage Manager
8:15 AM	Photographer arrives	Church	Photographer
8:30 AM	Church opens	Church	Wedding Stage Manager
8:30 AM	set up begins	Church	wedding party
8:15 AM	Bride and Groom Leave for Church	Church	Couple
8:45 AM	Photographer leaves for venue	Church	Photographer
8:45 AM	sound system check	Church	Wedding Singer
9:00 AM	Photographer arrives for photos	Church	Photographer + Couple
9:15 AM	Family Arrives for photos	Church	Wedding Party & Family
9:30 AM	Family Photos	Church	Photographer + Family + Couple
9:30 AM	flowers set up at Chruch	Church	Florist
9:50 AM	Wedding party photos	Church	Couple
10:30 AM	Reception set up begins	Venue	wedding party
11:30 AM	Final Wedding Touch ups Minister Arrives	Church	Minister and wedding party family
11:45 AM	Usher's take their places and begin seating	Church	ushers
12:15 PM	Guests are all seated and Wedding Party in Place	Church	all
12:20 PM	Wedding Ceremony	Church	all
1:00 PM	Couple + Wedding Party get ready	Getting Ready Area	Couple + Wedding Party

Day of Wedding Schedule Tool

Cocktail Hour			
1:30 PM	Couple Quiet time	take a walk	couple
1:55 PM	cocktail hour	venue	Wedding Stage Manager/ caterer
2:00 PM	Couple Photos	venue	photog, couple
2:15 PM	Couple joins party	venue	couple
Reception			
10:00 AM	cake picked up from bakery	bakery address	Reception Manager
2:30 PM	guest seated for brunch	venue	Wedding Stage Manager/ caterer
3:00 PM	toasts - four total	dance floor	names of toast givers
4:15 PM	meal over	venue	Wedding Stage Manager/ caterer
5:00 PM	first dance	dance floor	couple
5:35 PM	dance Bride and Dad Groom and Mom	dance floor	all
6:00 PM	cake cutting	venue	Wedding Stage Manager cues
6:05 PM	dance	dance floor	all
11:30 PM	last call	venue	announced by Wedding Stage Manager
11:45 PM	Send off	venue	Wedding Stage Manager cues
12:00 PM	guests out	venue	Wedding Stage Manager cues
Post-Reception			
5:00 PM	caterer & family start breakdown	venue	caterer/ family
10- 12:30 PM	families leave with stuff they're taking	venue	family
1:00 AM	breakdown done, everyone out	venue	all

These are only present as an example. Electronic versions of this spreadsheet are available upon request at **products@newbizplaybook.com**

Flower Options for Weddings

Wedding

Bride's Flowers

Bride's bouquet
Bride's floral crown or hair flowers

Groom Flowers

Groom's boutonniere
Groomsmens' boutonnieres

Wedding Party Flowers

Bridesmaids' bouquets
Flower girl's bouquet or basket of pedals
Ring bearer's boutonniere
Mother of the bride's corsage
Mother of the groom's corsage
Father of the bride's boutonniere
Father of the groom's boutonniere
Grandmothers' corsages
Grandfathers' boutonnieres
Officiant's boutonniere
Ushers' boutonnieres

Ceremony Flowers

Entryway or welcome table arrangements
Altar/chuppah arrangements
Pew or chair arrangements
Candles
Aisle decorations
Tossing petals for guests

Reception Flowers

Reception tossing bouquet
Cocktail table arrangements
Bar arrangements
Escort-card table arrangements
Centerpieces
Bride's and groom's chair decorations
Buffet-table/food-station arrangements
Lounge area arrangements
Flowers for wedding cake
Cake table arrangements
Powder room decorations
Getaway car arrangements

DJ Reception Planning Tool

Agenda:

6:00 PM Guests Arrive.   Background   music   begins.   Specify
Background Music _____

6:15 PM   Introduction of the Wedding Party. Do you want
                       to have your DJ announce your initial entrance
                       into the reception? If so who,

6:30 PM   Bride/Groom Arrive

6:45 PM   Cocktails: Decide   between   Classical,   Jazz,
                       Traditional   New   Age,   Classic   Soft   Rock,
                       Contemporary Soft Rock, (Bach, Vivaldi, etc.),
                       (Brubeck, Basie), (Sinatra, Martin, etc.), (Yanni,
                       Enya), (Billy Joel, Elton John, etc.), (Jack Johnson,
                       Jason Mraz, Colbie Caillat, etc.)

7:00 PM   The best man's toast is traditionally done
                       immediately before dinner, but can be done at
                       any time. Please let us know if the father of the
                       bride, the groom, or anyone else wants to say a
                       few short words of welcome.

7:15 PM   Blessing is traditionally done immediately after the
                       toast, and before the dinner is served. If there is a
                       blessing,

7:30   Dinner: Classical, Jazz, Traditional New Age, Classic
                       Soft Rock, Contemporary Soft Rock, (Bach, Vivaldi,
                       etc.), (Brubeck, Basie), (Sinatra, Martin, etc.),
                       (Yanni, Enya), (Billy Joel, Elton John, etc.), (Jack
                       Johnson, Jason Mraz, Colbie Caillat, etc.)

8:15 PM   Traditional Dances. The traditional first dances of
                 the evening will open up the dance floor, after
                 which your guests will be able to dance for the
                 rest of the evening. Typically, you will want to wait
                 until a time when most of your guests are almost
                 through with dinner. Please check off the dances
                 you would like to include, as well as indicating
                 which songs you would like to use for them.

Bride and Groom First Dance Song Title: _____Artist:_____

Bride/Father Song Title: _____ Artist: _____

Groom/Mother Song Title: _____ Artist: _____

Wedding Party Song Title: _____Artist:_____

All members of wedding party will dance (parents optional). Some
may invite all guests to join ½ way through the song to kick off the
dancing. Dance Music Begins.

8:30PM   Cake Cutting. When will you be cutting the cake?
                 Please circle one: As you enter Before Dinner After
                 Dinner

                 Do you want a special song played at this time?
                 Title:
                 _____Artist:_____
                 Would you like us to announce the cake cutting?
                 Yes No

9:00PM   Bouquet and Garter Toss. Typically, if a couple chooses to throw the bouquet and/or the garter, they will wait at least 30 minutes after the last Traditional Dance to do so. Background music is usually played while the DJ calls the girls out for the bouquet and if the groom will throw the garter, a fun song is usually played while it is being removed.

         Bouquet Song Title: _____Artist:_____

         Garter Song Title:_____ Artist:_____

9:30PM   Dollar Dance. As with the bouquet and garter toss, the dollar dance usually happens at least 30 minutes after the last Traditional Dance or immediately after the bouquet and garter toss. The dollar dance is optional.

DJ Details

What style DJ do you want: Quiet (no interaction during dancing) Moderate (interaction only if necessary) Outgoing (lots of interaction)

Is it more important for you to hear your favorite music, or for your guests to be dancing? _____

How many crowd-involvement songs would you like played (Electric Slide, Duck Dance, Cha Cha Slide, Cupid Shuffle, Anniversary Dance, etc.)?

These questions asked of your client will help to frame the experience they can expect from their DJ.

Bar/Bat Mitzvah

Bar/Bat Mitzvah Timetable
Start Planning Early!

Event Date: _____

2 Years Before the Event
- [ ] Obtain date from Temple/Synagogue.
- [ ] Set your budget.
- [ ] Decide on the type of event you want (day, evening, formal etc.).
- [ ] Estimate number of guests and book reception hall or caterer.
- [ ] Book the photographer/videographer.

1 1/2 Years Before the Event
- [ ] Book the DJ/band.
- [ ] Decide on your party theme and color scheme.

6-12 Months Before the Event
- [ ] Your child will start formal lessons/training
- [ ] Talk to florists about prices and floral designs.
- [ ] Decide on centerpieces/balloon designs.
- [ ] Start looking at invitation designs and prices.

6-8 Months Before the Event
- [ ] Book a hotel block for out-of-town guests.
- [ ] Start clothes shopping.
- [ ] Send out "Save the Date" reminders

3-6 Months Before the Event
- [ ] Order or design your sign-in board and guest book.
- [ ] Order favors.
- [ ] Order yarmulkes.
- [ ] Order your invitations.

3 Months Before the Event
- [ ] Finalize guest list.
- [ ] Make a hotel packet for out-of-towners.
- [ ] Try to make your final selections on clothing and accessories.
- [ ] Buy stamps.

- [ ] Have completely assembled invitations weighed to ensure correct postage.
- [ ] Find a calligrapher.

6-8 Weeks Before the Event
- [ ] Mail the invitations.
- [ ] Make up a song list for the DJ/band.
- [ ] Make appointments with florists/balloonist and place your order.

1 Month before the Event
- [ ] Make hair stylist and manicure appointments.
- [ ] Have final fittings done for clothing.
- [ ] Arrange catering for brunch.

2-3 Weeks before the Event
- [ ] Choose people for Aliyot and honors.
- [ ] Choose the people to be honored for the candle lighting ceremony and write poems.
- [ ] Meet with the DJ/band and make sure they know the candle lighting songs.
- [ ] Do guest seating arrangements and send to the reception hall.
- [ ] Order the food for Kiddush or Oneg Shabbat.
- [ ] Make sure the arrangements are complete with centerpieces, balloons, sign-in board, etc.
- [ ] Write prayers or speeches.
- [ ] Send final instructions to photographer/videographer.
- [ ] Pay all Synagogue fees.

1 Week before the Event
- [ ] Take formal pictures and pictures on Bimah.
- [ ] Meet with the caterer to finalize guest count.
- [ ] Make arrangements to get your guests from the airport to the hotel.
- [ ] Confirm your brunch arrangements.

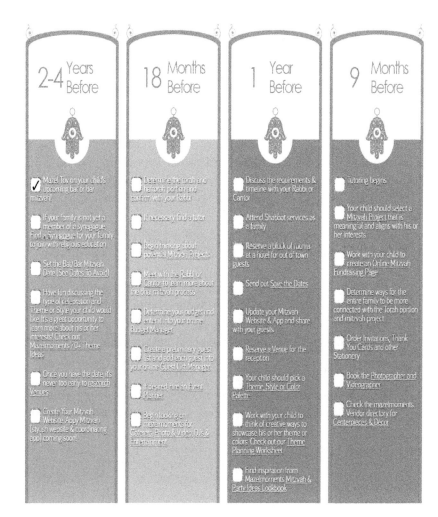

2-4 Years Before

- ✓ Mazel Tov on your child's upcoming bat or bar mitzvah!
- If your family is not yet a member of a synagogue, find a synagogue for your family to join with religious education
- Set the Bat/Bar Mitzvah Date (See Dates To Avoid)
- Have fun discussing the type of celebration and Theme or Style your child would like. It's a great opportunity to learn more about his or her interests! Check out Mazelmoments 70+ Theme Ideas
- Once you have the date, it's never too early to research Venues
- Create Your Mitzvah Website, App (Mitzvah stylish website & coordinating app) coming soon!

18 Months Before

- Determine the torah and haftorah portion and confirm with your Rabbi
- If necessary find a tutor
- Begin thinking about potential Mitzvah Projects
- Meet with the Rabbi or Cantor to learn more about the bnai mitzvah process
- Determine your budget and enter it into your online Budget Manager
- Create a preliminary guest list and add each guest into your online Guest List Manager
- If desired, hire an Event Planner
- Begin looking on mazelmoments for Caterers, Photo & Video, DJs & Entertainment

1 Year Before

- Discuss the requirements & timeline with your Rabbi or Cantor
- Attend Shabbat services as a family
- Reserve a block of rooms at a hotel for out of town guests
- Send out Save the Dates
- Update your Mitzvah Website & App and share with your guests
- Reserve a Venue for the reception
- Your child should pick a Theme, Style or Color Palette
- Work with your child to think of creative ways to showcase his or her theme or colors. Check out our Theme Planning Worksheet
- Find inspiration from Mazelmoments Mitzvah & Party Ideas Lookbook

9 Months Before

- Tutoring begins
- Your child should select a Mitzvah Project that is meaningful and aligns with his or her interests
- Work with your child to create an Online Mitzvah Fundraising Page
- Determine ways for the entire family to be more connected with the Torah portion and mitzvah project
- Order Invitations, Thank You Cards and other Stationery
- Book the Photographer and Videographer
- Check the mazelmoments Vendor directory for Centerpieces & Décor

Cost Projections

One of the first questions you will have or get from those who hire you is how to plan for costs of a Bar/Bat Mitzvah.

The following is meant to be a guideline. Keep in mind that if you are planning this event for hire, you may be charging by the hour ($75-$350 per hour is not uncommon), as a percentage of the cost of the event (10-20% is the typical range here), or if you have the venue and are hosting in your own location, you may simply charge a total price. This will impact client costs, and should be taken into consideration.

Invitations will range from 1-5 dollars depending on whether they are custom printed, design used and quantity ordered

Catering ranges from a low of $15 dollars per adult to more than $100 depending upon the food, whether the venue is included, and the number of people. This would not include a high end tiered cake, which will cost between $1-3 dollars per slice.

Venues can vary widely nationwide, and even in particular areas, depending on peak times. Expect to pay between $500 and $2500 for most venues, and with a larger group that number can get much higher.

Entertainment Costs are as follows:

DJ $500 - $1500 depending upon the amount of time, and whether additional light packages, extra sound equipment (such as karaoke), etc. are requested. DJ's are recommended for most parties as bands may have less ability to entertain the group which is very likely to be quite diverse at these events.

Magicians, and other party hosts that provide party or arcade games usually start in the $400 range and go up depending upon the request. Given that young children are very often in attendance at these events, balloon animals and other forms of entertainment may be popular.

Donations for the Rabbi(s) and Cantor – Different temples will vary, and some will have a Bar Mitzvah fee for hosting the celebration. It is common for such donations to be given to the Rabbi's discretionary fund. Some donors give in increments of 18 the multiple of chai, though it is not required. These donations are a function of the personal circumstances of the family however they are approached.

Extras

Flowers – These range from simple arrangements that can be obtained for less than $500, to more elaborate decorations that rival the cost of weddings in the $2000-$4000 range.

Gifts for attendees – They can be thoughtful photo packages of the child, which are less expensive, or t-shirts and more that add up. These are absolutely a function of your preference.

Manicures, Pedicures, Hair and Makeup – Don't ignore these as they will add up during your Bat Mitzvah.

Very often activities will be planned that also double as gifts for the kids in attendance. Examples of these include photo booths, candy making bars, wax hands, design your own flip flops etc.,

Industry estimates show that typical Bar/Bat Mitzvah's cost between $15,000 and $30,000 dollars, but these numbers are skewed as many families choose to host their own events, and privately subcontract catering etc., which wouldn't involve the "industry," much at all.

We have attached a simple budget tool here, but can send an electronic version upon request to products@newbizplaybook.com

Service or Vendor	Estimated Cost	Actual Cost	Deposit Due	Balance Due
Banquet Hall				
Caterer & Bar				
DJ/Band				
Photography				
Videography				
Decorations				
Invitations/Postage				
Entertainment				
Florist				
Event Planner				
Favors & Gifts				
Judaica				
Clothing				
Cake				
Friday Night Oneg Shabbat				
Saturday Kiddush Luncheon				
Personal Expenses				
Rental Items				
Transportation				
Morning After Brunch				
Synagogue Fees/Officiant Fees				
Total	$0.00	$0.00		$0.00

Bar/Bat Mitzvah Reception Tool

Contact Information

Client name: Phone/Email:

Bar (boy) / Bat (girl) *(circle one)* Mitzvah name:

Reception Date: Setup Start Time:

Entertainment Start Time: End Time:

The following is a typical but optional sequence of events.
The specifics should be coordinated with relevant venders
such as caterers, and DJ's etc.

Sequence	Time	Event
		Guests Arrive
		Cocktail Hour
		Main Reception Starts (guests join each other in main hall)
		Family Entrance
		Candle Lighting
		Hora
		Kiddush
		Motzi
		Toasts
		Salad within 30 minutes of entrance
		Guest of Honor/Parent Dance
		Main Course
		Host/Hostess Dance
		Dessert
		Open Dancing
		Finale

Venue Information

There are other tools in this publication for helping you to interview, plan for, and qualify the venue for your event. Those may be used here, so for example, there is a guest tracker in the wedding section. You may want to use something different for this event, but that will work here.

Name/address of establishment:

Contact name: Phone:

Primary room name/location:

Planning Logistics

Number of guests: Children:

Day School Guest of Honor attends: Hebrew School Guest of Honor attends:

Party Theme:

Number of courses to be served (including dessert):

Will the caterer be using the dance floor for a buffet during the cocktail hour? During the main course?

Contact Information for Other Party Professionals

	Name	Phone	email	Booked From_ to _
Caterer	Grande Dining Cuisine	(123)456-789	abc@def.com	7-9:30
Banquet Hall/Venue				
Planner/Coordinator				
Photographer				
Videographer				
Entertainer				

Cocktail Hour Planning Tool

Is cocktail hour in same room as main reception?   If not, what room is it in?

Music for cocktail hour:
Reception Start (Guests enter main reception room from cocktail room)

Music to start with (high-energy dance music recommended):

Reception Grand Entrance / Introductions

Who will be performing the introductions?

Suggested order of introductions:

1.   Parents (usually introduced as Host and Hostess, Bob and Jane)

2.   Siblings

3.   Guest of Honor

Re songs requested, if not review DJ reference tool for a feel about requests on music options, and DJ style preferences.

Please list those to be introduced during the grand entrance in the order they will be introduced. You can choose different songs for each person or one for the entire group. Use additional sheets if necessary. If you want, interesting tidbits of information about relationships to the guest of honor can be announced—if so, please write details below each person's name.

For each name collect:

Name(s)

Phonetic Pronunciation(s)

How to Introduce

Music

Candle lighting

A memory candle for deceased relative(s) may be lit by the guest of honor. Typically this is announced by the Guest of Honor, and is done either before the first candle is announced, or before the parents' candle is announced. Alternatively, one of the candles on the cake can be lit as a memory candle—this would be announced at the time of that candle. Will there be a memory candle?

Include the names of people who will be coming to the cake. Write the names as the Guest of Honor calls them and include phonetic pronunciation. The usual order for candle lighting is

1.   Grandparents
2.   Aunts
3.   Uncles
4.   Cousins
5.   Older relatives
6.   Younger relatives
7.   Friends of parents
8.   Friends of Guest of Honor
9.   Parents
10.   Siblings
11.   Guest of Honor

The usual number of candles is 14 *(13 for age, one for good luck)*. Try to group relatives and friends together to keep the amount of candles to 14 as best as possible. You can have interesting tidbits of information announced as the individuals come up to light the candles. If you want to do this, please write details below each person's name.

You will also need to choose music to be played while people come up and light the candles. You can have one piece of music serve as background to all of the candles or you may want to match a specific song to each person or group of people lighting the candle (*preferably fun and upbeat*). The total ceremony takes about 15 minutes.

Candle Lighting List

	Name(s)	Phonetic Pronunciation(s)	How to Introduce	Music
1.				
2.				
3.				
4.				
5.				
6.				

Events

Hora

Please indicate which family members you would like to be lifted in the chair during the Hora:

Kiddush

Who will be introduced to say the Kiddush blessing? Write the name as the Guest of Honor would, and include phonetic pronunciation.
Motzi

Who will be introduced to say the Motzi blessing? Write the name as the Guest of Honor would, and include phonetic pronunciation.

Toast

Who will be introduced to offer the toast to the Guest of Honor? Typically this is the father. Write the name as the Guest of Honor would, and include phonetic pronunciation.
Will there be other people offering toasts? If so, describe:

After the toast, will the Guest of Honor want to say something? This is a wonderful opportunity to welcome everyone and to do any special acknowledgements, such as guests who have traveled a long distance or friends or family who have contributed in the preparation of the ceremony or reception. This is a fun and memorable alternative to the typical, time-consuming receiving line.

Host/Hostess Dance

Song for host/hostess dance:
You can have us invite your guests to join in partway through the above song, or we can invite them up when the next song begins. When do you want us to invite other guests to join in?

Guest of Honor/Parent Dance

Song for guest of honor/parent dance (we recommend a slow song, some suggestions follow):

After which course (typically after main course):
You can have us invite your guests to join in partway through the above song, or we can invite them up when the next song begins. We can have all fathers/daughters and mothers/sons join you first and invite the rest of the guests to join in one verse later, or we can invite all of the guests to join in at the same time. When and how do you want us to invite other guests to join in?

For some people, a special dance with a Stepfather, Uncle, Brother, or close family friend is done in lieu of, or in addition to, a parents dance.

Grand Finale

Before the last dance, we can organize guests into a circle around the guest of honor, pass the mic around, and allow them to each offer best wishes. Do you want to do this?

Table Photos/Interviews

Please indicate the points (if any) during the reception when you and your photographer want everyone to remain seated for table photos:

Please indicate the points (if any) during the reception when you and your videographer want everyone to remain seated for table interviews:

If the photographer or videographer requests it, do you want us to clear the dance floor or delay the start of dancing for the completion of table photos and/or interviews?

Additional setups require:
Dedications, Birthdays, Anniversaries, Other Special Dances, etc.
List any special announcements you would like us to make. This is a great way to personalize your event and recognize someone special.

Additional Notes *(Use back or additional sheets if necessary)*
If there is anything else we need to know to ensure your reception flows smoothly, please list the details here. In particular:

- If you feel we need to be aware of Any sensitive information regarding your event, family, or guests
- If you are having a video presentation, a singer, musicians, fraternity/sorority serenade, centerpiece giveaway, or any other personalized additions that will make your party unique

Bar/Bat Mitzvah Gift Ideas

(Be sure to send the gift before you go to the event because it will take place on Shabbat)

1. Siddur (prayer book)
2. Chumash (Bible)
3. Shabbat Candlesticks
4. Silver Kiddush cup,
5. Yad (pointer used during Torah reading)
6. Havdalah Set
7. Tzedakah (box for charity to encourage giving)
8. Nice watch
9. Hamsa charms
10. Star of David, Chai, or Religiously themed jewelry
11. Wool Bnei or Tallit
12. Cash or gift certificates in increments of 18

Popular Bar/Bat Mitzvah Themes

Boys

Popular colors – Blue, Black, Silver, Gold, and Sports Team Colors

Themes – Sports, Action and Super heroes, technology, video games

Girls

Popular colors – Pinks, Purples, Blue, Grey, Green

Themes – Candy (as in Dylan's Candy Bar), Teen Club/Dance, Movies, and Travel

Quinceaneras

Cost Projections

One of the first questions you will have or get from those who hire you is how to plan for costs of a Quinceanera.

The following is meant to be a guideline. Keep in mind that if you are planning this event for hire, you may be charging by the hour ($75-$350 per hour is not uncommon), as a percentage of the cost of the event (10-20% is the typical range here), or if you have the venue and are hosting in your own location, you may simply charge a total price. This will impact client costs, and should be taken into consideration.

Custom invitations will range from 1-5 dollars depending on whether they are specially printed, the design used, and the quantity ordered. For those on a budget, custom invitations are available in bulk for as little as 70 cents each. If you choose this option, we recommend that you order examples early to ensure that the product meets your expectations. (see inviteshop.com)

Professional catering ranges from a low of $15 dollars per adult to more than $100 depending upon the food, whether the venue is included, and the number of people. This would not include a high end tiered cake, which will cost between $1-3 dollars per slice. If friends and family are helping to prepare the food, I have seen creative folks get that cost to between $2.50 and $3.00 a person using traditional Spanish and Mexican dishes.

Venue costs can vary widely nationwide, and even in particular areas, depending on peak times. Expect to pay between $500 and $2500 for most venues, and with a larger group that number can get much higher. If the Venue is one that is owned by a friend or family, you can often save a lot of money. If you plan to have your party outside, consider lining up tent rental, as weather can kill your event if you are not careful. Tent rental can range from 1-3 dollars per square foot including installation and delivery, so you may not be saving as much as you think.

Entertainment Costs are as follows:

DJ $500 - $1500 depending upon the amount of time, and whether additional light packages, extra sound equipment (such as karaoke), etc. are requested. DJ's are recommended for most parties as bands may have less ability to entertain the group which is very likely to be quite diverse at these events. Obviously, with the ability to store massive amounts of music on phones and tablets, and with the advent of high quality inexpensive DJ apps, music can be provided at a very low cost. This is harder than it looks. If a friend or family member is going to help here, they should practice, and plan the music playlist, or your event will definitely feel the difference.

If small children are involved, face painters, magicians, and other party hosts that provide party or arcade games usually start in the $400 range and go up depending upon the request. Balloon animals and other forms of entertainment may be also be popular. Some of this can be easily done by friends and family with just a little practice. Simple face painting ideas are easily available online.

Extras

Flowers – These range from simple arrangements that can be obtained for less than $500, to more elaborate decorations that rival the cost of weddings in the $2000-$4000 range.

Gifts for attendees – They can be thoughtful photo packages of the quest of honor, or a simply made photo booth with props, which are less expensive, or t-shirts and more that add up. These are absolutely a function of your preference.

Manicures, Pedicures, Hair and Makeup – Don't ignore these as they will add up during your Quinceanera, though they are fun for daughter, sister, mother, and grandmother to do together.

Very often activities will be planned that also double as gifts for the kids in attendance. Examples of these include, candy making bars, wax hands, design your own flip flops etc.,

Industry estimates show that typical Quinceanera cost between $5,000 and $20,000 dollars, but these numbers are skewed as many families choose to host their own events, and privately subcontract catering etc., which wouldn't involve the "industry," much at all.

We have attached a simple budget tool here, but can send an electronic version upon request to products@newbizplaybook.com

Service or Vendor	Estimated Cost	Actual Cost	Deposit Due	Balance Due
Banquet Hall				
Caterer & Bar				
DJ/Band				
Photography				
Videography				
Decorations				
Invitations/Postage				
Entertainment				
Florist				
Event Planner				
Favors & Gifts				
Clothing				
Cake				
Personal Expenses				
Rental Items				
Transportation				
Morning After Brunch				
Total	$0.00	$0.00		$0.00

Quinceanera Planning Checklist

The following is meant to be fully inclusive. There are likely to be items that you do not need or want, or that are not in your budget for the event you are planning. If you are planning an event for hire, be sure to involve the family in making sure that any special family traditions for Quinceanera get handled. It is not uncommon for families to be so caught up in the celebration aspect of this event, that they become distracted. No one wants to ruin this special time by finding out that a special piece of family history was not honored when it is too late.

1+ Year Before Quinceanera

- ○ Book the Church
- ○ Book the Venue
- ○ Consider options for Damas & Chambelanes of the Court
- ○ If applicable consider who your sponsors, madrinas and padrinos could be
- ○ Book Photographer or Videographer
- ○ If a special Priest or Minister is wanted involve that person early
- ○ Hire Event Planner if needed
- ○ Consider catering, DJ's and Entertainment
- ○ Begin to Formalize themes

9 – 12 Months Before Quinceanera

- Decide on final Damas & Chambelanes
- Decide on final Damas & Chabelanes suits and dresses
- Select invitations, and floral arrangements
- Determine any special traditions to be honored such as the changing of shoes or last doll (symbolizing the transition into adulthood).
- Block rooms for out of town guests at a desirable hotel
- Finalize themes
- Order favors (dolls, shoes, crowns)
- Decide and choreograph any special dances the court may want to do together
- Book any rental items such as chairs, tents, or tables
- Finalize guest list
- Order invitations
- Audition and Book DJ/Entertainment
- Interview Photographer (questions included below)

6-9 Months Before Quinceanera

- Make Hotel Package with addresses, phone numbers and details for out of town guests
- Confirm rentals if renting tents, tables, chairs, chair covers etc.,
- Get invitations completed and assembled.
- Make transportation arrangements as needed for guests with no cars, or elderly who cannot drive
- Submit photos for a video montage set to music to play at the party if desired
- Make Hair and makeup appointments
- Order cake or deserts if not provided by caterer
- Select Limousine or Car company and book if applicable

- Re-confirm all church arrangements

1-2 Months Before Quinceanera

- Mail the invitations
- Submit music preferences or special songs to DJ
- Dress alterations and Suit/Tux Fittings
- Quinceanera prepares her welcome/thank you speech
- Pay for flowers, photographers, and provide deposits as required
- Obtain Bible, Prayer Book, Cross, Rosary, Scepter and other items suiting your traditions
- Finalize song list
- Finalize seating arrangements
- Purchase gifts for members of Quinceanera's Court
- Formal Photo of Quinceanera in her dress for display at the event
- Buy or put together gifts received book for thank you letters and memories

2-4 Weeks Before the Quinceanera

- Confirm quest list for non-responders
- Confirm head counts with Venue and Caterer
- Finalize prayers, speeches, or toasts
- Finalize and re-confirm all details with bakers, photographer, florist, and pay deposits as required – provide special requests for family photos to be taken
- Dance rehearsals, and final dress fitting

1 Week Before the Quinceanera

- Confirm brunch arrangements if needed
- Confirm hair and makeup appointments
- Make final payments to vendors
- Finalize seating chart
- Have a rehearsal at the Synagogue or Temple

Day of the Quinceanera

- 8-10:30 am — Hair and Makeup
- 10:30-11 am — Get Dressed
- 12-1:30 pm — Mass Ceremony (Pictures at Church)
- 2:30-3:30pm — Pictures at Beach, Park, Special places
- 4:00pm — Guests start arriving
- 4:30pm — Grand Entrance
- 4:30-5pm — Toasts from parents, padrinos etc.
- 5-7:00pm — Welcome from Quinceanera/Dinner
- 7-7:30pm — Change of Shoes & Last Doll
- 7:30-7:45pm — Father Daughter Dance
- 8:00-8:30pm — Quince Waltz or Surprise Dance
- 8:30-9:00pm — Cake Cutting/Serving
- 9:00-12:00 — Party Down!

Quinceanera Reception Planning Tool

Contact Information
Client name: Phone/Email:
Quinceanera name:
Reception Date: Setup Start Time:
Entertainment Start Time: End Time:

The following is a typical but optional sequence of events.
The specifics should be coordinated with relevant venders
such as caterers, and DJ's etc.

Sequence	Time	Event
		Caterer Arrives begins setup
		DJ Arrives sets up and begins to play
		Main Reception Starts (guests join each other in main hall)
		Family Entrance
		Grand Entrance
		Toast
		Dinner
		Change of Shoes and Last Doll
		Father Daughter Dance
		Quince Waltz/Surprise Dance
		Guest of Honor/Parent Dance
		Cake Cutting
		Open Dancing
		Finale

Venue Information

There are other tools in this publication for helping you to interview, plan for, and qualify the venue for your event. Those may be used here, so for example, there is a guest tracker in the wedding section. You may want to use something different for this event, but that will work here.

Name/address of establishment:

Contact name: Phone:

Primary room name/location:

Planning Logistics

Number of guests: Children:

Party Theme:

Number of courses to be served (including dessert):

Will the caterer be using the dance floor for a buffet during the cocktail hour?   During the main course?

Contact Information for Other Party Professionals

	Name	Phone	email	Booked From_ to _
Caterer	Grande Dining Cuisine	(123)456-789	abc@def.com	7-9:30
Banquet Hall/Venue				
Planner/Coordinator				
Photographer				
Videographer				
Entertainer				

Cocktail Hour Planning Tool

Is cocktail hour in same room as main reception?   If not, what room is it in?

Music for cocktail hour:
Reception Start (Guests enter main reception room from cocktail room)

Music to start with (high-energy dance music recommended):

Reception Grand Entrance / Introductions

Who will be performing the introductions?

Suggested order of introductions:

1.   Parents (usually introduced as Host and Hostess, Bob and Jane)

2.   Siblings

3.   Guest of Honor

Re songs requested, if not review DJ reference tool for a feel about requests on music options, and DJ style preferences.

Please list those to be introduced during the grand entrance in the order they will be introduced. You can choose different songs for each person or one for the entire group. Use additional sheets if necessary. If you want, interesting tidbits of information about relationships to the guest of honor can be announced—if so, please write details below each person's name.

For each name collect:

Name(s)

Phonetic Pronunciation(s)

How to Introduce

Music

Candle lighting

This is a special ceremony in which the Quinceanera takes time to honor those who have been important in her live, by selecting 15 people, including parents, siblings, other family, and close friends. During the ceremony she dedicates a candle to each of those she has chosen, and as she lights each, the DJ plays a special song. When all candles are lit, she delivers them to those in attendance, while telling the guests why this person is so special in her life. For special people who have passed, the Quinceanera leaves their candles in place, lit as a reminder that these special folks are still with her, and she celebrates their impact in her life with those in attendance.

Include the names of people who will be involved

1.   Grandparents
2.   Aunts
3.   Uncles
4.   Cousins
5.   Older relatives
6.   Younger relatives
7.   Friends of parents
9.   Siblings
10.   Guests of Honor
11.   Parents

Symbolic Gifts

Many families choose the moment of her Quinceanera to celebrate a daughter's coming of age with special gifts. Common gifts include:

1. Bible
2. Rosary
3. Cross or Medal
4. 15 Roses
5. Tiara and Scepter
6. Special family jewelry or heirlooms

Changing of the Shoes and The Last Doll

A common tradition shared with a father and daughter, or if the father has passed or is not around, a grandfather, or older brother.

The Quinceanera is seated, and the father removes her shoes, changing them for different, more mature shoes. A doll is also offered to the girl, her last doll, in recognition of her transition to adulthood. Some families have ribbons pinned to the doll that the Quinceanera shares with her quests, as a way of insuring that she has thanked all in attendance. In some families, the Quinceanera presents that doll to a younger sibling as a special gift.

Celebrating Sponsors and Guests of Honor

It is very common in latin cultures for parents to pay for part of the Quinceanera celebration, and to have help from friends and family, often called sponsors.

This is a highly respected role in the celebration, and time is often taken to thank these sponsors, where the Quinceanera publicly shows her gratitude, and recognizes them for the honors they have bestowed upon her.

This is done at different times, and is handled in the traditional manner of a toast.

Candle Lighting List

Name(s)	Phonetic Pronunciation(s)	How to Introduce	Music
1.			
2.			
3.			
4.			
5.			
6.			

Grand Finale

Before the last dance, we can organize guests into a circle around the guest of honor, pass the mic around, and allow them to each offer best wishes. Do you want to do this?

Table Photos/Interviews

Please indicate the points (if any) during the reception when you and your photographer want everyone to remain seated for table photos:

Please indicate the points (if any) during the reception when you and your videographer want everyone to remain seated for table interviews:

If the photographer or videographer requests it, do you want us to clear the dance floor or delay the start of dancing for the completion of table photos and/or interviews?

Additional setups require:
Dedications, Birthdays, Anniversaries, Other Special Dances, etc.
List any special announcements you would like us to make. This is a great way to personalize your event and recognize someone special.

Additional Notes *(Use back or additional sheets if necessary)*
If there is anything else we need to know to ensure your reception flows smoothly, please list the details here. In particular:

- If you feel we need to be aware of Any sensitive information regarding your event, family, or guests
- If you are having a video presentation, a singer, musicians, fraternity/sorority serenade, centerpiece giveaway, or any other personalized additions that will make your party unique

Quinceanera Theme Ideas

1. Hollywood
2. Fairytale (with colors chosen from famous stories)
3. Mardi Gras
4. Candy land (used for decorations and to add color that fits the pallet chosen by the quinceanera)
5. Masquerade
6. Renaissance
7. Carnival
8. Under the Sea
9. Dios De Los Muertos
10. Traditional Western
11. Fiesta
12. Bohemian
13. Great Gatsby Roaring 20's
14. Charro
15. Enchanted Forest/Evening
16. Winter Wonderland
17. Beauty and the Beast
18. A Night in Paris
19. Flamenco
20. Black and White Ball

Quinceanera Invitation Template

Mr. Martin Montenegro & Mrs. Maria Montenegro

-Are pleased to invite you -

To the Celebration of The Fifteenth
Birthday of Their Daughter

Celeste Montenegro

The holy mass in her honor will take place:
Saturday August 18th, 2017 at 11:00 a.m.
Saint Helen's Catholic Church
1010 Buck Street, Houston, TX

Please RSVP by 5/5/17 to Rosa Garcia at
222-222-2222 or rosa@madeupemail.com

Chamberlain of Honor
Jose Rodriguez

Damas	*Chamberlains*
Stephanie Smith	*Jesus Rebenga*
Giselle Sanchez	*Alex Rodriquez*
Laura Avalos	*Jorge Avalos*
Ashley Montalvo	*Luis Cisneros*

Large Conference Planning Budget Tool

While not easily depicted in print, we have built a spreadsheet tool to assist in tracking costs and budgets for a large conference, based on a number of factors including number of attendees at **products@newbizplaybook.com**.

	#	$	subtotals	Estimated Total	Actual Total	change +/-
AV Equipment & Stage						
AV Breakouts:	4	$500	$2,000			$0.00
AV General:			$0			$0.00
Set:			$0			$0.00
Labor			$0			$0.00
Stage			$0			$0.00
Video Production			$0	$2,000		-$2,000.00
Venue Rental Fees						
Rental			$0			$0.00
Business Center			$0			$0.00
Set Up			$0			$0.00
Permits			$0			$0.00
Misc (biz center etc.)			$0			$0.00
Clean Up			$0			$0.00

Food & Beverage

Cocktail Party:	$0	$0.00
Monday	$0	$0.00
Tuesday	$0	$0.00
Wednesday	$0	$0.00
Thursday	$0	$0.00
Friday	$0	$0.00
	$0	$0.00
Meals:	$0	$0.00
Monday	$0	$0.00
Tuesday	$0	$0.00
Wednesday	$0	$0.00
Thursday	$0	$0.00
Friday	$0	$0.00
Marketing Team Dinner	$0	$0.00
Meals		$0.00
Décor *(bill to dept xyz)*		$0.00

Category	Amount	Subtotal	Total
Offsite Night			
Party	$0		$0.00
Talent @ party	$0		$0.00
Gifts	$0		$0.00
Food & Drink	$0	$0	$0.00
			$0.00
Transportation			$0.00
Agency Fee	$0		$0.00
Air	$0		$0.00
Shuttles	$0		$0.00
Auto	$0		$0.00
Buses/Limos	$0	$0	$0.00
			$0.00
Hotel Rooms			$0.00
Lodging Single Rooms	$0		$0.00
Lodging Double Rooms	$0		$0.00
Lodging Suites	$0		$0.00
Pre-Conference Rooms	$0		$0.00
Staff Rooms	$0		$0.00
Site Inspection	$0	$0	$0.00

Creative/Collateral			
Design Fees			$0	$0.00
Placement Fees			$0	$0.00
Design			$0	$0.00
Main Gift - herbie			$0	$0.00
Notebooks			$0	$0.00
Brochures			$0	$0.00
Napkins			$0	$0.00
Centerpeices			$0	$0.00
Luggage Tags			$0	$0.00
Scrims			$0	$0.00
Disposable Cameras			$0	$0.00
Team Shirts			$0	$0.00
Invites			$0	$0.00
Photographer			$0	$0.00
Pillow Gifts			$0	$0.00
Chocolates			$0	$0.00
Decorations	0	$0	$0	$0.00
Stage Furniture			$0	$0.00
Printing - Signage				$0.00
Badges - Domestic			$0	$0.00
Badges - Intl			$0	$0.00

Signage Design	$0		$0.00
Signage Printing	$0		$0.00
Program	$0	$0	$0.00
			$0.00
Guest Speakers	$0		$0.00
Travel Expenses	$0		$0.00
Spa/golf	$0		$0.00
Speaker Gifts	$0		$0.00
Wine/Cheese to rooms	$0	$0	$0.00
			$0.00
			$0.00
			$0.00
Event Labor			$0.00
Registration Helpers	$0		$0.00
Uniforms	$0		$0.00
	$0	$0	$0.00
			$0.00
			$0.00
			$0.00
Other Expense - Domestic	$0		$0.00
Receiving boxes/delivery	$0		$0.00
Tips to Hotel	$0	$0	$0.00
			$0.00

Customer Tracking Tool

Customer Name	Phone	Email	Address	Last Contacted	Last Ordered	Notes

Event Signage Planning Tool

Wording	number	size	placement location	placement 2	notes
Agenda	2	18x34	outside classroom	next to registration	final version due X date for printing
Breakfast	3	8x11			make clear food set out is for this event
Lunch	3	8x11			place in plastic stands
Event Name +"Registration"	3	16x20	top of stairwell	bottom of stairwell	include arrow pointing right on one/left on other/none on the third
Phone Booth	2	8x11	outside floor one phone booth		logo of old fashion phone and event logo
Registration A-G	1	16x20	above registration		May need to HANG from ceiling
Registration H-P	1	16x20	above registration		May need to HANG from ceiling
Registration Q-Z	1	16x20			
Restrooms	2	11x14	foyer	on ground floor	include arrow pointing right
Restrooms	2	8x4	place on bathroom door		clever branding opportunity
Welcome (incorporate logo)	2	16x20	inside meeting room entry (on easels)		
Cocktail Party	2	18x34	outside of tent on easels	in parking lot	include arrow for parking lot
Specialty Drink Descriptions	2	8.5x11	on bars in plastic holders		
Attendee Gifts	1	11x14	outside meeting room at 5pm		
Event Logo (purely branding)	2	16x20	in front of meeting hall doors	next to valet	need arrows pointing UP
Vertical Banners	2	3x8	placed outside meeting room after program		vinyl and free standing, BLR Sign Systems
Podium Sign	1	16x20	mounted on podium		
(speaker names) on large place cards	12	tent cards	on stage chairs		print with Avery tent card paper on computer

Event Wrap Closeout Tool

As an event planner, it is very important to close out your events with detailed information you can use for future reference in the event you seek to use the facility for future events.

Name of Event:
Date:
Chair/Event Producer: Your name or the event chair
Executive Host: sr. exec that served as the internal champion
Location: name of venue, city, state

BUDGET
Event Budget: Total allotted event budget
Actual Budget: $
Any Major Overruns & Reason: good to know
Outstanding Payments/Issues: list any disputes, outstanding major bills that may be en route, hopefully this is blank

MARKET
Target Audience: such as: Chief Marketing Officers from consumer packaged goods companies in the mid-west region.
Number of Invitations Sent:
Number of Attendees:
Actual Attendance demographics: EX: 8 CMOs, 4 CEOs, 14 EVPs, 26 Directors. Or for a country club: 37 Current Members, 43 Recruits
Highest Ranking Attendee: Name, Title, Company

COMMUNICATIONS
Hard Copy Invitation: Invitations sent 10 weeks in advance, tri-fold style, sent to 1200 invitees

Email Invitation: Soft copy invitation was sent from Liz Champaign 5 weeks before the event and again 3 weeks before the event to all who had not yet RSVP'd. Design created by Firefox Communications.

Confirmation Method: All attendees were sent a confirmation email immediately after they registered on the event website. All attendees also received a phone call confirmation one week before the event to answer questions and confirm participation.

Recommendations for future invitations to this event: What would you do differently? Send fewer/more, different style, change the frequency of communication?

***If you can, you'll probably benefit from pasting a copy of the email invitation and a scan of the hard copy invitation to the end of this document.

SURVEY SUMMARY:

Highest scored speaker:

Lowest scored speaker:

Suspected reason:

Most attended breakout:

Least attended breakout:

Most popular activity:

HOTEL

Room Block Numbers: 14 Suites, 109 Singles, 5 Doubles all days

Actual Usage/day: 13 Suites, 115 Singles, 4 Doubles on Tuesday

No Shows: 3 Tuesday, 6 Wednesday, 10 Thursday

Rate: $265 Suites, $119 Singles, $144 Doubles/night

ACTIVITIES

Golf: 84 Signed up/96 Showed

Tennis: 48 Signed up/36 Showed

Hiking: 22 Signed up/19 Showed

Recommendations:

EVENT STAFF

Number for Event: 14 onsite staff members, 6 were from J&J Temps

Number recommended for next year: Example: We would benefit from four more hosts at the golf tournament check in and a few more during the cocktail party registration desk.

Quotes from Clients/Attendees:

Share some great testimonials here received verbally or via email post event that your team, execs or future planners would enjoy hearing.

Final recommendations for next event:

Photos:
Add a few photos of the event that help jog your memory the next time around or help the next person. Centerpieces, signage, registration tables and stage sets are great to keep on file.

Golf Events

Here are some ideas for hosting a great golf event!

Driving Contest

- Place judges on this fairway to cheer on your guests and keep score of the drives
- The pro can mark off milestones with flags prior to the Tournament beginning
- Each player gets three to five drives
- The top three drives count
- Works best on a long, wide, flat fairway

Longest Drive

- Guests who may not be accurate can show off their strength and ability to drive that ball down the fairway
- Works best on a par-5, long fairway

Shortest Drive
- Short is good in this case.
- Use the same par-5 hole as the longest drive contest, allowing more "winners"

Straightest Drive
- White line is placed down the middle of the fairway.
- The ball that lands on, or closest to, the white line is the winner.

Closest to the Pin
- Shot that comes to rest closest to the pin.
- Typically seen on a par-3 hole on the second half of the Tourney.

Longest Put
- Tiger Woods? Select a green with a challenging lie.
- Guests can place their ball as far out as they like, others then try to beat the leader.
- Works well as a pre-game contest, prior to play, great way for your guests to warm-up with friendly banter.
- If you have the budget, this is a great contest to pair with a marquee prize – the "Thousand Dollar Putt" or "Putt for a Buick".

Made in the USA
Las Vegas, NV
02 January 2022

40022125R00075